ALONE
on the
COLORADO

This undated photograph of Harold Leich was taken around the time of his Colorado River trip. Photograph courtesy of the Harold Leich family.

ALONE
on the
COLORADO

HAROLD H. LEICH

foreword by
ROY WEBB

THE UNIVERSITY OF UTAH PRESS
SALT LAKE CITY

The Defiance House Man colophon is a registered trademark of The University of Utah Press. It is based on a four-foot-tall Ancient Puebloan pictograph (late PIII) near Glen Canyon, Utah.

 Copublished with the Special Collections-Tanner Trust Fund, J. Willard Marriott Library.

Library of Congress Cataloging-in-Publication Data

Names: Leich, Harold H., author. | Webb, Roy, writer of foreword.
Title: Alone on the Colorado / Harold H. Leich ; with foreword by Roy Webb.
Description: Salt Lake City : The University of Utah Press, [2019] |
    Identifiers: LCCN 2018047511 (print) | LCCN 2018049220 (ebook) | ISBN
    9781607816775 | ISBN 9781607816768 (pbk. : alk. paper)
Subjects: LCSH: Leich, Harold H.—Travel—Colorado River (Colo.-Mexico) |
    Colorado River (Colo.-Mexico)—Description and travel.
Classification: LCC F788 (ebook) | LCC F788 .L45 2019 (print) | DDC
    917.91/304—dc23
LC record available at https://lccn.loc.gov/2018047511

Permission acknowledgments

All photographs were taken by Harold H. Leich except as noted. Photographs used courtesy of Harold M. Leich and Jeffrey R. Leich, from the Harold H. Leich collection located in Special Collections, J. Willard Marriott Library, University of Utah.

Printed and bound in the United States of America.

Errata and further information on this and other titles available online at UofUpress.com.

CONTENTS

FOREWORD BY ROY WEBB | *vii*

PREFACE | *xix*

CHAPTER ONE: *The Spell of Swift Water* | 1

CHAPTER TWO: *Bewitched* | 29

CHAPTER THREE: *The Source* | 39

CHAPTER FOUR: *In the Wake of Sam Adams* | 57

CHAPTER FIVE: *Idylls of a River Rat* | 73

CHAPTER SIX: *Swapping Horses in Midstream* | 97

CHAPTER SEVEN: *Ulysses (Junior Grade)* | 107

CHAPTER EIGHT: *Shipwrecked in the Desert* | 131

CHAPTER NINE: *Afoot and Afloat* | 147

CHAPTER TEN: *Hell or Hanksville* | 157

CHAPTER ELEVEN: *Farewell to the Colorado* | 169

AFTERWORD BY JEFF LEICH AND HARRY LEICH | 177

NOTES | 185

FOREWORD

Roy Webb

MUCH LIKE A RIVER meandering through a valley, I came to the story of Harold Leich in a roundabout way. After twenty years of research and writing about the history of travel by boat on the Green and Colorado Rivers, I was familiar with the name Harold Leich, but that was about all. Then early in my career as an archivist, I attended a meeting of the International Skiing History Association, held that year in Park City, Utah. As part of my position at the University of Utah I was on the board of the Utah Ski Archives, and so was introduced to a fit, athletic man about my own age named Jeffrey Leich, who was the director of the New England Ski Museum in New Hampshire. As we talked he asked me where I liked to ski, and I had to confess that I was the token non-skier on the board. I joked, as I always did in those moments, that I was more interested in floating on the melted snow as it ran down the Colorado River canyons. Oh, he said, my father ran the Colorado River in a kayak in 1933. At that moment I put the name Leich together with the Colorado River and listened with eager interest.

JEFF TOLD ME THE TALE of his father's adventures from the source of the Colorado River to Cataract Canyon, in the depths of Canyonlands National Park, including how he had taken a fragile kayak down the upper Colorado and then a wooden boat of his own design and construction the rest of the way. Hal, as he liked to be called (his sons remember that the first thing he would say when introduced to someone was "call me Hal," so that's what we'll do) made it as far as Cataract Canyon before his boat was wrecked and he was forced to make his way out of the canyon—no small feat even in today's age of GPS and high-tech hiking gear. But happily his travel journals survived, as well as photographs, letters, and other memorabilia, including his waterproof folder from Abercrombie and Fitch to protect those journals. In his later years, Hal wrote several different versions of a book-length manuscript about both his experiences on the Colorado River and traveling the West during the Great Depression, and those were also part of the collection. I was very excited to hear of this treasure trove, and asked Jeff if he would be interested in depositing his father's papers with the Utah River Running Archives at the University of Utah's Marriott Library. After he consulted with the rest of the Leich family, they agreed, and now Harold's legacy is available to the public and researchers. It's from that legacy that the present book issues forth like the river we started with and enters the next canyon after long looping meanders through a broad valley.

In *Alone on the Colorado*, Harold Leich's charming and detailed manuscript, his spirit and passion for the river come through so strongly that he needs little further introduction. Suffice to say he was born by a great river in Indiana in 1909, the end of the age of steamboats on the Ohio and Mississippi Rivers. Those early days set Hal on an adventurous course for the rest of his life. He came of age during the Great Depression and joined the ranks of thousands of uprooted Americans looking for work or a new life. But far from a tale of despair, Hal's journal records that he seemed to thrive on riding the rails, sleeping in hobo camps, spending brief spells as a traveling salesman and repairman, and working on a small steamer up and down the coasts of America. After learning about the Yellowstone River in a local library, where Hal "spent all of my time, and none of my money," he built a small boat and floated over two hundred miles of the Yellowstone through Montana, on his way from the Pacific Coast to Indiana. It was that successful trip, as well as another book in another library, that gave him the inspiration and confidence to run the Colorado River. The Colorado River voyage—first in a "battered" Klepper folding kayak he bought from a German in Cincinnati and named the *Rob Roy* in honor of the boat used by a nineteenth-century Scottish adventurer, and then in the *Dirty Devil*, a small wooden punt he built in Grand Junction, Colorado, named for a small tributary of the Colorado below Glen Canyon—from Grand

Lake to the unexpected end of his boat journey in Cataract Canyon, comprises the majority of *Alone on the Colorado*. "The truth of the matter," Hal wrote, "is that I was drugged—bewitched—by a roaring golden river 2,000 miles away that I had never even seen," and modern readers will be equally entranced by a story written almost a century ago by a young man of whom most have never heard.

Since Hal's tale is so well-told, this foreword serves to set the stage for his voyage and bring the modern reader up to date on changes along the Colorado River. The Colorado River starts in truly "grand" surroundings, in the Never Summer mountain range, now part of Rocky Mountain National Park. A small, clear body of water surrounded by towering snowy peaks, Grand Lake is listed as the official source of the Colorado River.[1] The town of Grand Lake is much changed from 1933, when Hal started his voyage. It's still a tourist town and the historic district looks much the same, but the hot dog shops and tourist traps he described have been replaced by a new public library and vacation homes and condos all the way around the lake. Hal describes paddling the Colorado through a broad valley below the outlet of Grand Lake. This was Middle Park, the historic gathering place of Native Americans, trappers, ranchers, and miners. Most of this stretch of the Colorado is now submerged under a series of reservoirs—Shadow Mountain, Lake Granby, and Windy Gap—that were all constructed since his journey to divert water from the upper Colorado to Denver and the Front Range, on the other side of the Rockies.

At Granby, Colorado, the Fraser River joins the Colorado. The Fraser is the first of many large tributaries that contribute to the flow of the main river. Below Granby, the Colorado has sculpted a narrow valley lined with ranches and fields, mostly unchanged from when Leich went through. Hal's next stop was the town of Hot Sulphur Springs—then, as now, dependent on visitors to the hot springs, although today recreational river running boosts the local economy. Byers Canyon, which starts right below town, is the first of many canyons carved by the Colorado with varying degrees of climate, grandeur, and difficulty of travel. A low canyon of red walls, Byers contains a number of small rapids that seemed difficult to Harold Leich, and the ranchers and railroad workers Hal encountered warned him of certain death if he tried to paddle through Byers Canyon. They all remembered Beppo Saeckler, a German kayaker, who preceded Hal through Byers Canyon in 1930. Saeckler started on the Fraser River at Granby, after traveling across America by boat, but only made it as far as Byers Canyon before he wrecked his kayak. After recuperating for some time in Burns, Saeckler continued his voyage, but after he left Grand Junction he was not heard from again. Today Byers Canyon is the upper end of a very popular stretch of river, run annually by thousands of people from all over the country.

Hal next encountered the Blue River, another large tributary that joins the main Colorado at Kremmling, a small ranching and tourist town. Sam Adams, a nineteenth-century Colorado booster and fabulist, began his misbegotten exploration of the upper Colorado on the Blue River in 1869, after he was rebuffed by John Wesley Powell. Adams thought he should be in charge of Powell's expedition down the Green River, but Powell sent him packing, recognizing someone possessed of more bluster than competence. Undaunted, Adams persuaded the citizens of Breckenridge, Colorado, to finance an expedition down the Colorado River. They launched with four boats and much fanfare from the town—including an embroidered banner made by the ladies of Breckenridge—but within a few days Adams had lost all his boats and supplies, so he limped back to Breckenridge and obscurity.

Below Kremmling the Colorado River gets serious, beginning to earn the dangerous reputation it has carried for hundreds of years. Gore Canyon, with some of the most difficult whitewater rapids in North America, was named for a nineteenth-century Irish tourist, Sir George Gore. Gore hunted the area extensively in the 1850s, killing thousands of bison and a great deal of other wildlife. The canyon that bears his name is, perhaps fittingly, a deep, gloomy slash in the mountains that looks like the setting for a scene from a Tolkien novel. Gore Canyon's rapids were made much worse by the building of the Denver and Rio Grande Western Railroad from 1903–1907. As the crews blasted away the rock cliffs, they shoved the boulders into the river just below them, creating dangerous cataracts full of sharp-edged boulders. Hal Leich carried his boat around many of the rapids in Gore Canyon, but it wasn't until the 1960s that running the canyon was attempted again, this time by another German, Walter Kirshbaum. And it wasn't until the late 1970s before Walt Blackadar and Roger Paris, (prounounced "Rog-et Par-ee") a champion French kayaker, ran the whole canyon without a portage. Today Gore Canyon is run by expert kayakers and other boaters on a regular basis, and the Gore Canyon Whitewater Festival is attended by thousands every year who come to witness expert boaters test their skills in the still-intimidating whitewater. Those festival-goers, along with passengers and workers on the Union Pacific trains that still pass through the canyon, are the only ones who can watch the competition, as a highway has never been built through Gore Canyon.

BELOW GORE CANYON the Colorado runs through small canyons and open valleys, passing small hamlets like Bond, Burns, and Radium. Today these towns depend largely on both the recreational boaters who flock to the area and the railroad. Besides the railroad, a gravel road follows the river in many stretches. Except for a few improvements on the road and the railroad—including the completion of the Dotsero cutoff of the Moffat Road in 1934—the area looks much the same as when Hal paddled through in August 1933. Hal met many of the workers on the cutoff, which connected Denver and Salt Lake City by rail; he stayed with them, obtained supplies and help from them when needed, and shared stories of the raiload. But when the cutoff was completed the next year, the construction camps were shut down and today the area is largely deserted.

At Dotsero, Colorado, the Eagle River joins the main stem, but more significantly, the Colorado also meets Interstate 70, finished in 1992 to connect Denver to I-15 in Utah. Immediately below Dotsero the river enters Glenwood Canyon, which was already obstructed by a dam and diversion built in 1909 to provide electrical power. This dam was the first of many that have obstructed the river's course, but the construction of I-70 created much bigger rapids than Hal would have faced. The canyon is so narrow above Glenwood Springs that the eastbound and westbound lanes of the freeway had to be cantilevered over each other, and even today the highway is often narrowed—and sometimes closed—by rockfalls. Although upper Glenwood Canyon is now a playground for boaters and tourists, it has been the scene of tragedy. In May 1956, three men from Glenwood Springs attempted to run the canyon in a war-surplus pontoon, the inflatable craft then being adapted for river running all over the west. The water was high, fast, and cold, however, and the men were soon thrown into the river when the boat capsized. One escaped unscathed, another was injured, but the third, Bob Mann, drowned. His body was recovered sometime later at Rifle, Colorado.

By the time Hal passed through the town of Glenwood Springs, it was already well-established as a stop on the railroad and a destination for tourists and those seeking a cure in the hot springs. Today visitors still flock to the steaming, spring-fed pools, but now the town is also a gateway to the world-renowned ski areas around Aspen, Colorado, and a center of commercial river running on the easy stretches below the Shoshone dam. Then, as if weary of canyons and rapids for a while, the Colorado flows in a broad, arid valley below Glenwood Springs and through Rifle, Silt, and Parachute, small towns that were once supply centers for local ranches and have gone through periodic oil and gas booms from the 1970s to the present. At De Beque, Colorado, the Grand Valley Diversion Dam—a low, "roller" dam—was built in 1916 to funnel water using canals and ditches to the rich bottomlands along the Colorado in Palisade and Grand Junction. Hal would find the dam unchanged to this day, still carrying out its original function. The canals fed by the dam supply Colorado River water for the entire Grand Valley, from Palisade, Colorado, through Grand Junction almost to the Utah border. Fruit and wine from orchards and vineyards that line the river comprise a major part of the local economy.

Grand Junction, Colorado, a small farming and railroad town where Hal paused to build a new boat (the *Dirty Devil*) and regroup for the canyons and deserts he knew lay below, has grown to be Colorado's largest city west of the Rocky Mountains. Today it has over sixty thousand people and is a center for oil and gas production, mining, ranching and agriculture, service industries, and medical facilities. Colorado National Monument and many national forests and Bureau of Land Management areas contribute to the local economy, as do a number of medical centers and hospitals. Grand Junction was named for the confluence of the Gunnison and Colorado Rivers, Gunnison being both the largest and the last tributary of the Colorado within the state.

Below Grand Junction the river begins to cut through the Colorado Plateau, a high, arid upthrust of sandstone that leaves the river bound by deep canyons for most of the rest of its length before joining with the Green River in what is now Canyonlands National Park. Crossing the Colorado-Utah border, the river flows through two short, low sandstone canyons: Horsethief and Ruby. Easy rapids, beautiful scenery, and big camping beaches make this a favorite for modern boaters, and today this part of the river is heavily used by rafters from Colorado and Utah. The railroad follows the Colorado in Horsethief and Ruby Canyons, leaving the river at

Westwater. From that point on there is only one short stretch of highway paralleling the rest of Hal's route.

When Hal floated through in 1933, there were still several small railroad stops along the river where people lived and worked. Westwater, Cisco, and others were hamlets where workers on the railroad and their families lived, but today they are all ghost towns, so there are fewer people living along the river than when he paddled through. Just below the mouth of Ruby Canyon, Westwater Canyon cuts through dense Precambrian metamorphic rock, sometimes called Black Canyon schist (which Hal mistakenly identifies as igneous), creating continuous, challenging rapids that are now the delight of whitewater enthusiasts. In Leich's day, though, the locals in the small rail towns warned him against attempting Westwater Canyon, telling him grisly tales of drownings and near-death experiences. And for once, they were not exaggerating; according to Westwater Canyon historian Mike Milligan, by the time Leich took the *Dirty Devil* through Westwater's seventeen miles of rapids, a number of people had drowned and others had come to various stages of grief attempting to float the canyon.[2] Milligan believes that one of those who was lost in the canyon was Beppo Saeckler, the German kayaker last seen resting at a farm in Burns, Colorado, after wrecking his kayak in Byers Canyon a few years before Hal Leich. The dangerous rapid where Leich described how "the entire river tilted onto a huge tilted slab" and half of the river "curled back to the right, swirling in a narrow pool beneath the vertical wall" is today known as Skull Rapid—the whirlpool has earned the name the Room of Doom, and the rapid been the scene of more than one accident. But despite—or perhaps because of—the dangers, today a permit to run Westwater Canyon is one of the most highly prized among Colorado River boaters.

The Little Dolores River joins the Colorado at the head of Westwater Canyon, while the main Dolores River joins just after the end; these are the last major tributaries of the Colorado before it meets the Green River. Below the mouth of the Dolores, the river enters a long scenic stretch of spectacular sandstone canyons leading to Moab, Utah. This part of the river flows past Fisher Towers and borders Arches National Park, and has long been an avenue of travel both up and down the river since the rapids are small. Timber was floated down the Colorado from the LaSal Mountains to Moab, while in the early twentieth century steamboats traveled on the river above and below the town. Starting in the 1940s and continuing to the present, numerous movies were made along this part of the Colorado, with Professor Valley and Fisher Towers as a background for films, television shows, and commercials. Hal Leich saw no one else on the river when he floated it in 1933, but today commercial river outfitters in Moab send thousands of happy tourists down this splashy, scenic stretch every year. When he passed through, there was only a primitive trail along the river leading to the Dewey Bridge, constructed in 1916 to connect Moab and the railroad at Cisco, and the road remained mostly unpaved until the 1970s. Now the primitive trail that Hal saw has become Utah Highway 128, listed as a scenic byway, and the entire length of the river through these canyons is a recreation area with campgrounds, hiking and bicycle trails, boat launches, and even a pair of popular resorts.

Moab, Utah—Harold Leich's last stop before he entered the remote canyons that are now within Canyonlands National Park—had a population of just over three hundred when he stayed at the Peterson Ranch, on the south side of the old highway bridge. Moab had been gradually settled since the 1870s by cowboys, ranchers, and farmers, unlike the rest of Utah, which had been colonized by the Church of Jesus Christ of Latter-day Saints. It was a tiny hamlet with one main street and a few small businesses, but still a center of settlement in the area. Of all the places along the river he visited, Moab has changed the most. The Peterson Ranch, the Bush lumberyard where he made new oars, the orchards and fields, and the farms and shops where he bought supplies for the next leg of his voyage have been replaced by hotels, restaurants, bicycle and recreational vehicle shops, and other businesses that cater to the tens of thousands of tourists from all over the world that visit Moab every year. However, the sudden growth spurt that Moab went through in the 1980s when it became a recreation powerhouse was not its first. About a dozen years after Leich passed through, the U.S. government began buying uranium, found in abundance all around Moab. The uranium frenzy that occurred from the late 1940s through the 1970s sent Moab's population skyrocketing from three hundred to over eight thousand. The uranium boom crashed in the 1980s, but the creation of Arches and Canyonlands National Parks as well as Dead Horse State Park allowed Moab to rebrand itself as the center of a thriving recreational economy.

From Moab down to Glen Canyon, the Colorado flows in deep, multi-hued sandstone canyons. The entrance to Meander Canyon—from Moab to the confluence of the Green River in Canyonlands National Park—is called "the Portal," an imposing narrow gate into the canyon world. A short stretch of highway parallels the river, but after it ends there are no more towns, bridges, or even roads for miles. In the early twentieth century, ambitious locals tried to establish steamboat travel between Moab and the small rail town of Green River, Utah. Moab, like Grand Junction, had a good climate for growing fruit, but there was no way to transport it to the railroad. Steamboats and other paddle-wheel craft seemed the answer, and although there were a number of attempts, the only one to successfully travel up and down the river was the *Undine*, a small gasoline-powered paddle wheeler. It was wrecked above Moab, at the Big Bend, in 1909. Hal noted the abandoned oil wells along the river below Moab, which had been drilled in the 1920s. The Baldwin Brothers, who ran the Moab Garage, used powered barges to transport people and supplies downriver to the oil wells, orchards, and ranches below Moab. By the time Hal floated through, the steamboat days were over, the oil wells shut down—one after a spectacular fire in 1925 that burned for days—and the fields and ranches abandoned. In the years after his voyage, uranium miners prospected down the river, cutting precipitous bulldozer trails high into the cliffs, and a giant uranium processing mill was built just below the modern highway bridge. A huge potash mine was started in the 1960s and still ships the mineral on a railroad line built specifically for that purpose. And from the late 1960s through the 1970s the Colorado River Marathon, a powerboat race, was run from Green River, Utah, down the Green River and back up the Colorado to Moab. This event attracted hundreds of powerboats, and the canyons reverberated with throbbing high-powered motors. The marathon, also known as the Friendship Cruise, ended with the low water years of the late 1970s, but large powerboats are still used for tours and shuttling river runners who canoe down the Green River through Labyrinth and Stillwater Canyons.

Cataract Canyon, where Hal lost his boat, is below the junction of the Green and Colorado Rivers. Cataract is a deep, narrow canyon, the channel blocked by limestone boulders that have washed and tumbled from the cliffs above. Now part of Canyonlands National Park, the miles of big rapids in Cataract Canyon were once known as the graveyard of the Colorado because so many boats were lost trying to navigate the cataracts. Following the discovery of gold in Glen Canyon in the 1890s, many prospectors lured in by the calm waters below Moab and Green River, Utah, disappeared in the rapids of Cataract Canyon. By the time Hal and the *Dirty Devil* came to grief in Cataract, a few expeditions had successfully worked their way through miles and miles of difficult rapids, but the canyon still retained its ominous reputation. Today's recreational boaters and tourists, however, are undeterred by Cataract Canyon's grim past, clamoring for permits to run the remaining rapids such as Little Niagara, Mile Long, and the Big Drops. The construction of Glen Canyon Dam, completed in 1963, flooded the lower end of Cataract Canyon and covered thirty miles of rapids, including the stretch where Hal lost his boat between Imperial and Waterhole Canyons.[3] The lake has since dropped, but the lower rapids remain covered by many feet of silt deposited by the turbid Green and Colorado Rivers.

Hite, Utah, which Hal reached by climbing, swimming, and slogging through mudflats for miles along the shores of Cataract and Narrow Canyons—on one shoe with two socks on the other foot—had once been an active community with several dozen inhabitants, a post office, a ferry across the river, and a store that supplied travelers, prospectors, and Navajo Indians. Cass Hite started a ferry there in the 1870s, and the gold boom in the 1890s brought a measure of prosperity to Hite. By the time Hal struggled down the rocky shores of Cataract Canyon to Hite, however, he found to his dismay that it was long abandoned, and would be for another decade. The ferry was reestablished in 1946 and Utah Highway 95 bulldozed down North Canyon. During the uranium boom of the 1940s and 1950s, a uranium mill was established in nearby White Canyon and there was once again a small community at Hite. But some three decades after Leich left Hite to trudge through the desert to Hanksville, Lake Powell—the reservoir behind the Glen Canyon Dam—covered both the little town and the ferry. A marina named after the original town of Hite opened to supply houseboats on Lake Powell, but after the lake started to drop in the 1990s, it too was abandoned.

The long, hot trek from Hite to Hanksville that took Harold Leich days to walk is now Utah Highway 95. It wasn't paved until 1976, but now tourists can drive in comfort from Hite to Hanksville in just over an hour on a modern two-lane highway, crossing the Colorado River on a soaring bridge. Hanksville, Utah, the tiny Mormon hamlet where Leich finally returned to civilization, remains much as he saw it. Today it subsists mostly on tourism centered around nearby Lake Powell and Capitol Reef National Park. Between Hanksville and Green River, Utah, just west of the long sandy path where Leich and his companions struggled in their Dodge sedan, the state of Utah has created Goblin Valley State Park, another major tourist draw. Green River itself is still a small town that ekes out an existence from agriculture, tourism, and supplying gas and snacks to travelers on I-70. The combination of a long growing season, sandy soil, and Green River water produces world-famous melons that are celebrated in an annual Melon Days festival. The railroad where Harold hopped on an eastbound freight still runs through the town, but the trains no longer stop there.

After Harold Leich caught that eastbound boxcar and headed back to his home in Indiana, he never returned to the west. As he noted in his manuscript, "for several years afterwards, in the late winter, I would draw plans for a new cataract boat and write up a grub list, but I never made the break again." Though Harold Leich never came back to the Colorado, he never forgot it. Relying on his diary salvaged from the wrecked boat, he wrote down his experiences in a lengthy manuscript. His closing words speak to how much being cast away on the Colorado affected him: "Today the canyon country seems as dim and shimmering as a Utah mesa fifty miles away on the noonday skyline. Like a Maxfield Parrish painting, filled with fair dreams and purple fantasies, the memory of the Colorado fades away to the far horizon."

Harold Leich went on to a successful career in civil service, raised a family, became a well-known expert in the field of wastewater management, and passed away in 1981. He remained very active outdoors, hiking, skiing, and canoeing around his home in Bethesda, Maryland. He was active in outdoor groups, including the Ski Club of Washington, D.C., the American Canoe Association, and the Potomac Appalachian Trail Club. Hal instilled in his sons Harold (Harry) and Jeff his own love of the outdoors and adventure. Harry became an archivist and specialist on Russian history at the University of Illinois and the Library of Congress, as well as a world traveler, while Jeff has spent his life and career "focused on skiing and the outdoors."

As we've seen, Harold Leich's 1933 journey down the Colorado is one of the most remarkable in the annals of American river exploration. He set out from Grand Lake on an unknown river with a modicum of experience and an inadequate boat, and yet persevered, learned, adapted his craft, and managed to do something no one else had done before him: run some of the most difficult whitewater and traverse some of the most remote country in North America, and, remarkably, return to write down his experiences. And yet at the same time, his journey is one of the least known. His manuscript was never published before today, and accounts of his journey were found only in old newspapers and a short article he wrote for the *Deseret News* in 1949.[4] His son Jeff described Harold's efforts to bring his story to light in a short biographical sketch:

> Hal began writing this book literally during the 1930 and 1933 river trips. Using a practice he followed most of his life, he wrote letters home on lined, hole-punched notebook paper. He also kept detailed notes on the same kind of paper and would later integrate these into a binder with his letters, retrieved from recipients, to form a detailed record of his adventures in chronological order.
>
> As his sons we remember, beginning in the 1950s, his evening trips to the basement to work on a book-length account of his adventures. This was inspired by an inquiry from Otis "Dock" Marston, the Colorado's legendary historian, which led to correspondence and a long friendship. Hal ultimately produced three complete versions, dated 1958, 1969, and 1978, all typed by him on a small manual typewriter. He used various titles and subtitles for the proposed book, including *Castaway on the Colorado*, *Rapids and Riffles*, and *Alone on the Colorado*. Hal made several attempts beginning in the early 1960s to find a publisher for his manuscript, but never succeeded. After his death, his second wife, Marian Nash, tried a number of times to locate a publisher, again without result.

Hal's failure to find a publisher for his manuscript was forgotten as his busy life and growing family turned his thoughts elsewhere. But now, thanks to his family, the Marriott Library Special Collections, and the University of Utah Press, Harold Leich's story of being cast away on the Colorado can finally get the attention it has so long deserved, and Harold can finally join the ranks of legendary early river runners, lured by the wild water and remote canyons of the Colorado River.[5]

PREFACE

In October 1956, I received a letter that began as follows:

Cataracteer Leich:

I have been on a long search for you but now I think this trek may be at an end.

I believe you once worked for General Foods in Cincinnati and that was when you were 25 years of age. Either in 1933 or 1934, and I think the latter, you started from Grand Lake in Colorado using a kayak to take you to Grand Junction . . .

My correspondent signed himself Dr. Otis Marston of Berkeley, California. By piecing together bits of information about my youthful escapade on the Colorado, this fluvial detective and Colorado River historian had tracked me down.

Far more than a historian of the river, Dock Marston has run the cataracts many times himself. To his interest I owe this effort to resurrect the past and to show how things were in the canyon country and elsewhere in the nation during the Great Depression.

CHAPTER ONE

The Spell of Swift Water

"Water always flows downhill, at a rate determined by the slope of the incline, subject to certain variations in the depth or width of the river bed. The color of the water, the setting of the stream, the sunlight dancing on the ripples, the mood of the observer—these have no interest for the scientist because of their idiosyncratic nature. But they are the chief concern of the poet."

—"A Poet Speaks," by Barriss Mills

THERE MUST BE A LITTLE of Huck Finn in most of us. As we stand on the bank of a rushing stream and watch the swift current suck at the willow roots and hear it gurgle in the eddies, a pioneering urge rises to the surface: the urge to drop the business of the day, push off aboard a raft, skiff, or anything that floats, and venture down the stream; to run the rapids around the next bend and camp on a sandbar at nightfall.

This urge must be imbedded in the ancestral memory of mankind, echoing the experiences of our forefathers of fifteen thousand years ago as they watched the great floods roaring down from the melting ice sheet and occasionally braved the current by log, raft, or coracle. And what rivers they must have been, far surpassing in volume the floods we know today! No wonder the silver surface of a rapid stream, heaving in motion and flecked by breaking crests, awakens a long-buried desire to climb aboard for a free ride on the tossing current.

In primeval days, swift water meant freedom—escape from an enemy, perhaps, or a chance to find better hunting grounds down the river. And swift water today means freedom too—the chance to roll downstream with the current out of the twentieth century into a wilderness of forest and crag, of clean water rippling in the sunlight, of heron and deer and beaver, even though a farm or a factory town may lie over the next hill. In a world of snarling traffic and screaming jet planes this is the kind of escape that we all need for physical and mental health—escape back through the centuries to the life of primitive man, to the ancient battle of muscle and wooden blade against reef and rapids.

I suppose I got more than my share of Huck Finn's love of the flowing current, growing up as I did in a river town. Evansville, in the southwestern tip of Indiana, owes its origin to the early settlers who pushed over the Alleghenies and came down the Ohio River by flatboat. The river was the chief geographic fact of my boyhood. The old house where I was born looked out across the Ohio to the low Kentucky shore. Every spring high water from the melting Allegheny snows covered the cornfields in the Kentucky bottomlands and the yellow current tugged at the wharf boat a few steps from our door.

Later we moved several blocks up the same street, near the water works. The big flood of 1913 filled the street, lapped close to the foundations of our new house, and rose in the cellar. The water works became an island surrounded by its levee, and we used to watch the changing shifts of workers rowing back and forth in a big river skiff.

In bad winters shanty boats tied up in the mouth of Bee Slough (pronounced "sloo" in southern Indiana), near the water works, to escape the grinding ice flows of the Ohio. An open sewer, Bee Slough was not quick to freeze. The boatmen led an idyllic life, floating with the current in summer, fishing a little, and tying up wherever the bank seemed inviting. One winter a boy from a shanty boat sat just ahead of me in Wheeler School. Every morning he would pull a smoked catfish from his pocket and eat it for a snack while the teacher opened the window for ventilation.

Our after-school group of my brothers, cousins, and friends ranged the river bank for a mile or two, from the water works down past the mouth of Bee Slough to the wharf boat in the center of town. This region was a wasteland of mudbanks, cinder piles, jimson weed thickets, and ragweed jungles, but it brought us to the wide, yellow rolling river whose waters drained a quarter of a continent and surged without a break to the Gulf of Mexico. Herring gulls that had followed the waters upstream from the ocean for a thousand miles wheeled and dived for catfish off Sunset Park. I used to argue with grownups who told me the gulls were just our old courthouse pigeons.

The wharf boat was permanently moored at the foot of Main Street, at the bottom of the Evansville levee. While everyone called the place a levee, it was not actually raised above the surrounding areas as the word implied. It was just a wide cobblestone beach sloping down into the river and extending about a half a mile along the waterfront. Teams of powerful sweating horses pulled drays of river cargo up the levee from the wharf boat to the warehouses on Water Street, which ran along the top of the levee and formed the first street of our town. The street was the occasional scene of razor affrays, which the *Courier* the next morning described as "cutting scrapes." As we hiked along Water Street our noses caught intriguing odors from tobacco shops, saloons, and liquor warehouses. When the wind was right the smell of fermenting malt came from the vats of two large breweries.

Bee Slough was the launching site of our first boat, a long packing case caulked with tar. We paddled her briskly through the sewage, but she was so cranky that we all agreed our next boat should have more beam. The second venture did not get out of the basement, since we made the classic error of forgetting to measure the width of the cellar door.

We grew up at the end of the steamboat era. The glamour and glory were dying fast, but for us there was no finer sight than the steamer *Evansville* racing downstream past the water works on her weekly voyages with passengers and hogs from remote landings on the Green River, which enters the Ohio a few miles above town. As she sped past us in the swift channel her enormous stern paddle wheel beat the river to yellow foam, the passengers waved to us from her gingerbread decks, the hogs squealed, and she sounded a deep blast of her steam whistle to warn the roustabouts on the wharf boat of her return. There came a sad time in the early 1920s when her twin black smokestacks, mounted abreast near the glass pilot house, were trimmed down to remove some ornate curlicues at the top. After that she seemed more like a work boat than a saucy river packet.

She was about the last of the old-fashioned steamboats sailing out of Evansville. The volume of river traffic today is heavier than ever, but the tall white sternwheelers have given way to squat diesel towboats pushing a city block of steel barges, all lashed together into one huge component. This new river life must have its own glamour; maneuvering such a lash-up around a sharp bend in a storm would be a challenge to Mark Twain himself.

Up into the 1920s Evansville wholesale houses depended on steamboats to carry goods to small river towns that were off the railroads and had not yet been reached by truck lines. Our family firm owned a few shares in the small *Bay Queen* for this purpose, and in the office hung a reminder of grander days: an oil painting of the majestic *Southland* in a storm. Various family connections had once piloted river steamers, and my father and his brothers in their early years made voyages by skiff to call on customers in river hamlets where the packet could not tarry long enough to allow a leisurely business call.

Sometimes on summer mornings we would hear the music of a steam calliope far down the river. If we were fast enough we could reach the levee in time to see a big excursion steamer make a landing, like the magnificent *St. Paul*, a visitor from the Mississippi River with three or four decks of white-painted gingerbread.

In winter drifting ice cakes threatened the thin-hulled river steamers and the fleet dispersed to safe harbors on side streams like the Green River. In the big winter of 1917–1918 the Ohio froze from bank to bank—a rare occurrence—and when the ice broke up that spring it piled into high ridges like the Yukon.

The deep-toned whistle of the water works blew the theme song of my boyhood. The town was still small enough to use the whistle as a fire alarm, and many a night we woke up to hear the slowly rising and falling sound across the cornfields. One night the sound did not cease but rose and fell repeatedly. Our father told us an ocean-going vessel had come up the river and was in distress. She proved to be an old sailing vessel advertised as the former British convict ship *Success*, a teak square-rigger of the eighteenth century that was being towed up the Ohio on exhibition. Whatever the cause of her distress, she moored safely at Sunset Park the next morning. We all went aboard to see wax figure exhibits of her supposed former inmates and such gruesome objects as the *Iron Maiden* and cat-o'-nine-tails. In later years the truth came out that, while ancient enough, she had actually been a peaceful merchantman.

About this time in our nation's literary history a pulp magazine called *Sea Stories* appeared on the newsstands, its columns filled with thrillers by Captain Dingle, H. Bedford-Jones, and similar writers. From the "pen pal" section in back, I began to correspond with Luds P. A. Cruelund, the harbor pilot of Aarhus, Denmark, who sent me dozens of photos of square-riggers under sail, mostly in Scandinavian waters, and clippings about the magnificent new Danish school ship, *Kobenhaven*, the last five-masted bark ever to be launched. She later went missing in the South Atlantic with a full complement of cadets and crew, and no trace of her has ever been found despite years of searching organized by the Danish government.

In high school days, I rode out of my way many mornings so I could pedal my bike along a cinder path in Sunset Park to watch the waves, the gulls, and the rapid current. In winter, I would ride into the teeth of the northwest wind in order to see the whitecaps kicked up in the current by the opposing wind. Sometimes they would become foaming breakers wild enough to sink a skiff. The path ran past the Coast Guard cutter *Kankakee* at her moorings, a trim sternwheeler that always kept up a head of steam for some river emergency and that often used it.

In warm weather the older boys who owned canoes would lie in wait for a steamboat to come along. They would shoot out towards the oncoming vessel, run close to its side, and swing into the wide wake behind the churning stern paddle wheel. The tossing waves, sometimes five or six feet high from trough to crest, would give them a roller-coaster ride and would frequently turn them over. Many years later I learned that the series of high crests behind a sternwheeler behave just like a chain of standing waves in a heavy river rapid.

I left the banks of the Ohio in September 1925 to enter Dartmouth College in the granite hills of northern New England. After growing up among the Indiana cornfields I was taken by the beauty of the countryside and spent every free moment out of doors. The swift brooks, fringed by white pines, ran clean over their gravel or rocky bottoms—quite a change from the sluggish sloughs and bayous along the Ohio. One afternoon I walked down to the Connecticut River and tested my canoeing skill in an effort to join the Ledyard Canoe Club, a group of sportsmen who took an annual cruise down the river to Long Island Sound. I didn't know the j-stroke, however, and since my bow wobbled from side to side I was blackballed. But fortunately, I knew how to walk in a straight line so the Dartmouth Outing Club let me in.

The log of my freshman trips shows that I spent almost every weekend on the trail, walking, skiing, and snowshoeing more than six hundred miles. During vacations, I spent more time in the hills than on visits home, sometimes skiing alone to mountain cabins. My English instructor, Evan Woodward, took his class to a cabin on a mountain pond where he read Robert Frost by firelight.

In the summers, I usually stayed in the north country, building or repairing cabins and cutting trails, and often helping out at the Moosilauke Summit Camp, a mountaintop hiking lodge on an outlying peak of the White Mountains. When the evening chores were done we would sing cowboy and hobo songs around the fireplace. One of them rang in my ears like a battle cry for years afterwards:

I've beat my way from Frisco Bay
To the rockbound coast of Maine,
From Canada to Mexico
And wandered back again.
I've met town clowns and harness bulls
As tough as a cop can be
And I've slept in every calaboose
In this land of liberty

During Christmas vacation of my senior year I spent a week working for Sherman Adams in a logging camp in the Pemigewasset Wilderness, grubbing out frozen soil and rocks for a logging road high on the snowy slopes of Mt. Bond. Ostensibly I was there collecting material for a term paper in my labor relations class, but actually I spent my evenings around the stove with seasoned hoboes learning the lore of the open road.

Four years of outdoor life turned me away from the river road to the wild scrub forests and granite crags of the high country. But these experiences set my feet on a winding trail that would lead to the river road again. I came out of college determined to knock around a while before following my classmates into the business world. Somehow the life of a logger, deckhand, or hobo seemed more attractive to me than a career as a bond salesman or production executive in the dingy factory cities that I passed on my way to and from college. At least I wanted to find out, and since I was only twenty on graduation I felt I had a year or two for experimentation.

Along with this feeling was a firm and arrogant belief in the virtue of going it alone on the trail or elsewhere, rather than getting mixed up with a lot of inexperienced companions who would just slow you down.

One might well ask why the expenditure of thousands of dollars on a college education had led to such an outcome. The answer would seem to be too many hours in the public library reading Charles Kingsley, Frederick Marryat, Robert Louis Stevenson, John Masefield, Mark Twain, Jack London, James B. Connolly, Dillon Wallace, Jim Tully, Bill Adams, and similar writers. Four years of climbing and skiing over the summits of the White and Green Mountains reinforced the impelling call of these spirits to be on my way, down to the sea or to the splendid wild regions of forests and mountains.

And so, in the late autumn of 1929, while my classmates were studying law at Harvard or hanging on to their first jobs as management trainees in the darkening depression, I was elated to land a berth as a deck boy aboard the intercoastal freighter *Sea Thrush* as she lay at a North River dock in Manhattan.

I must have looked more like a college boy than a deckhand when I reported aboard the *Sea Thrush* on the cold morning of December 3. The gaunt-faced Norwegian bosun ordered me to take off my tweed topcoat and shovel a fresh fall of snow off the high bridge amidships. Later in the morning we tightened the huge turnbuckles of the chains that lashed down our deckload of Douglas fir beams, carried around from the West Coast, and at noon we shifted berths down the river to Todd Basin, Brooklyn. Tugs and ferries came and went near our course. For an inland boy raised on the tales of William McFee, David T. Bone, and Joseph Conrad this was paradise indeed—to watch the maritime world at work and even take a small part in it, and to earn real money at that. My one dollar a day was all clear, since my bunk and meals were free.

For the first days aboard the *Sea Thrush* I led a dual life, leaving the ship when the day's work was done at 5:00 p.m. and going by subway to Hick Street, Brooklyn Heights, where I borrowed a bed from cousin Bob, a management trainee in the miscellaneous nut and bean department of a large importing house. We spent our evenings with his friends from Yale or my former roommates, and many an argument raged whether it was better to devote your youth to miscellaneous nuts and beans or to a free-ranging life afloat. Early each morning I put on my dungarees and caught the subway back to the world of shouting bosuns and rattling steam winches.

The oncoming depression had not yet affected the intercoastal trade. Many steamship lines owned fleets of freighters that spent their working lives shuttling between East and West Coasts through the Panama Canal, in a thriving trade that brought lumber from the Pacific Northwest and canned fruits and vegetables from California eastward and sent steel products, chemicals, and other manufactured goods back in the other direction. I remember seeing ships of the Luckenbach, Arrow, Sudden and Christiansen, and American-Hawaiian lines then engaged in this trade along with many others. The *Sea Thrush* belonged to the Shepard Line of Boston. Her sister ships were the *Wind Rush*, *Sage Brush*, and *Timber Rush*. Our crew speculated that the line could never become any larger because they had run out of names—the only remaining possibility being *Tooth Brush*.

The *Sea Thrush* was built during the First World War, and like hundreds of her sisters was about 5,400 tons in size and of the "three-island" type. That is, her silhouette formed three distinct islands from a distance: the raised forecastle ("focsle") at the bow; the midships structure with bridge, smokestack, quarters for officers, etc.; and then the raised poop at the stern. The crew's space was just beneath the poop deck, and by the ancient tradition of the sea was still called the forecastle, although misplaced by a ship's length. Slightly more than a decade old, the vessel was well maintained and modern for her day, although she would look archaic now with her angular lines and spindly smokestack.

Most of the men in our deck crew had sailed for many years. They still sang sea chanties when they came aboard after an evening on the town and spoke among themselves of the old days under canvas. To me they would say, "My boy, you will never see such fine ships again." Largely Scandinavian and Dutch, they were a decent and kindly crew when sober. I was treated almost like a son.

The *Sea Thrush* still had most of her West Coast cargo to discharge at eastern ports. I stood my first seagoing watch one evening as we passed the Narrows en route for New London. There we began unloading our lumber, but as the day went on we ran into unexpected difficulties. The bosun's voice, always hoarse, got much worse. He tried to shout until he got red in the face but we couldn't hear him ten feet away. Finally, when it came time to lower the cargo booms and secure the vessel for sea, he asked me to transmit his orders to the crew. I stood at his side while he whispered his commands and I shouted them forth as his mouthpiece: "Lower the starboard boom," "Secure no. 5 hatch cover," or "Stand by with heaving lines to receive tug on port side."

The next port was Boston and then we turned around and began the long voyage for the West Coast, first stopping in New York and Philadelphia for cargo. One evening the forecastle really boiled. The bosun and a seaman had been fired that afternoon and they hung around in the evening while a bottle passed back and forth. They persuaded two more men to quit with them, and the forecastle resounded to the classic song of a sailor's parting:

> The times are hard and the wages low—
> Leave her, bullies leave her.
> I guess it's time for us to go—
> It's time for us to leave her.

We entered the port of Philadelphia two mornings before Christmas, towing up the crowded Delaware through a blizzard. On the twenty-seventh we signed the West Coast articles in the ship's saloon and the following day cast loose at dark. While unmooring we nearly overturned our tugboat because we couldn't slack off the stern hawser fast enough when the tug and the ship strained apart. The tug crew used a fire axe to cut the eye of the big hawser in order to save themselves. We were delayed by fog in the lower river and then on the thirtieth passed the Delaware capes and stood out to sea for the West Coast.

The first few days on the open ocean convinced me that seafaring in the age of steam held about as much excitement as the life of a janitor or painter ashore. We spent most of our days chipping rusty decks or washing down painted bulkheads. The only sense of adventure for a deckhand was the wheel watch; this gave a feeling of mastery in controlling the five thousand-ton seagoing monster as it climbed the long swells and slid down the other side.

The ship's antiquated, steam-operated steering gear required quite a time for the bow to respond when the wheel was turned. Steering a reasonably straight course required nice timing and judgment; if the ship's head fell off a couple of degrees to the right of the compass course, the helmsman would turn the wheel to the left for a short interval to correct the heading. But if he kept the wheel left long enough to start the ship's head visibly back to the proper course he would overcompensate, swinging her far off course to the left. Thus, the man at the wheel had to outguess the ship, the wind, and the seaway to maintain a good course, and the wake he left behind told the officer on watch how good a job he was doing.

As we approached the Caribbean the wind increased, and steering became a fascinating exercise in judgment. Long rolling crests from off the port quarter would lift her stern and move it far to starboard, thus swinging the bow ten or twenty degrees off course to port before the helmsman could correct this violent motion.

On the fresh morning of January 4, 1930, we passed close to Castle Island, a storybook speck of green leaves and white beach surrounded by the sparkling Atlantic. The water faded from light green near the beach to deep blue offshore, while a lofty lighthouse of banded red and white completed the color scheme. The next day we passed through the Windward Passage into the Caribbean and sighted the misty, mountainous bulk of Haiti looming to the east. The best time of day as we cruised the Spanish Main came just after supper, when the deck gang and the engine room gang loafed on no. 5 hatch cover and listened to a portable phonograph.

We went through the Panama Canal on January 8, while the deck boys spent most of our time at the masthead looking at the scenery. Good weather continued along the west coast of Central America. Before going on watch each evening I would join the group on no. 5 hatch cover, and night after night the silver moon emerged from cloud banks along the rugged coast. In these evening sessions (as well as with the groups of working stiffs I later met on sea or land), by mutual consent no one questioned anyone else about his past. Sometimes information would be volunteered, but listeners were careful not to follow up much or press too hard. Given or last names were seldom used—most of us were readily identified by names related to appearance, such as "Whitey," "Red," "Pop," "Blackie," or "Shorty." Foreigners were often known by nationality—"Dutchy," "Swede," or "Frenchy." "Slim" was the name that followed me from ship to ship and camp to boxcar without my ever suggesting it—and occasionally "Big tall feller," although I missed six feet by an inch or so. As far as I knew, no one ever suspected I had gone to college.

On January 21, we saw the lights of San Pedro while I was on evening lookout, and I handled the wheel when we came to anchor behind the breakwater. I was glad to be on the West Coast and did not intend to return east with the *Sea Thrush*. My problem was to keep employed until the weather warmed up so I could sleep out and make my way home to Indiana, seeing the sights along the way. Therefore, I decided to stay with the ship as she shuttled up and down the coast, discharging her cargo and picking up her deckload for the next trip to New York.

From San Francisco we pointed north and on February 1 hove to off the Columbia River bar waiting for the fog to clear. On lookout that morning I saw a spectral vessel appear through the fog and resolve itself into the pilot boat. When my turn at the wheel came the fog lifted enough for us to get underway. Steering by the pilot's orders, I headed for the river entrance —"Port your helm . . . steady as you go . . . now starboard easy and steady up on the lightship." We seemed to go straight for the lightship for a long, long time, but then in a moment we turned towards the land and left her a few yards to port.

In my day, American merchant vessels still used the obsolete and confusing terminology of "helm" instead of "rudder" in orders to the man at the wheel. "Port your helm" meant that the ship's tiller, or helm, should go to the left—or port—side, meaning the rudder and consequently the ship should go to the right. Steering wheel, rudder, and ship all moved in the same direction while the helm moved in the opposite direction, and this was the key word on which the steering order was based! No wonder many an accident was blamed on this medieval practice, which went back to the days when the helmsman actually stood at a large tiller, before steering wheels were invented. As a result of bitter experience, the U.S. Navy had shifted to the clear-cut "right rudder" and "left rudder" many years before. In 1932 the British merchant marine changed over, and finally in 1935 Congress passed the Helm Order Act to put the American merchant fleet on a truer course.

One evening off the coast of Washington, while we were rolling in high seas, I caught a glimpse of what seafaring had been in the days of sail. Just before sunset we sighted a large four-masted schooner heading for the entrance to Gray's Harbor under shortened sail. This was the first time I had seen a large sailing vessel pitching and rolling in heavy weather at sea. Like a creature alive, she parted the waves and dipped and reared in the turbulent foam. Her reefed sails glowed in the last shafts of sunlight while the half-moon showed through tawny rolls of scud. This distant glimpse fulfilled all the expectations of my inland boyhood.

Back in San Francisco I left the *Sea Thrush* before she sailed for the East Coast, and found another berth aboard the *Pennsylvania*, just in from the Orient. I stayed with her until Portland and switched again to her sister ship, the *Illinois*, in order to stay on the West Coast until spring. One day's work in Portland harbor had a great influence on my later life. A redheaded Liverpool Irishman and I were painting numerals to show the vessel's draft at the bow and stern. We used a small wooden punt and in maneuvering her along the ship's waterline I got the idea of building a similar one to cruise down the Missouri River on my way back to Indiana. As it happened, some days later I found Lewis R. Freeman's book, *Down the Yellowstone*,[1] in the Portland public library, and therefore shifted the plan to take my inland cruise down the Yellowstone River in Montana.

Despite the growing economic depression, I succeeded in getting several shore jobs out of the Portland skid road—with a highway gang building culverts along the Siuslaw River, in a logging camp high in the Cascades, and on a dairy farm. Finally, warm weather came and I paid a farewell call to the Portland Public Library, where I had spent most of my spare time that spring and none of my money. With my old White Mountain packsack on my shoulders I headed out of town. After dozens of lifts on the highway and several hauls on freight trains, I reached Yellowstone Park in late May and soon landed a job as a "pearl diver" (i.e., dishwasher) at the Fishing Bridge cafeteria. On the truck ride through the park to my new duty station I met Mr. Hornbeck of Livingston, Montana, a carpenter who had grown up on the banks of the Yellowstone River. He encouraged me to try the river trip and offered to help me when I was ready to build the boat.

We reached the place just before supper. Old Billy, the crabby German cook, put me to work at once with Ed, the other helper, peeling spuds, waiting on tables, and washing dishes. The cafeteria fed thousands of tourists each summer, but long before the season opened it was feeding a gang of carpenters who were repairing the tourist cabins. The three of us did all the work of feeding this crew of thirty men, and we found it took us from 4:00 a.m. until 9 p.m., with a few hours off in the afternoon.

Ed and I slept on cots in the rear of the kitchen, next to the wall. Just over our heads hung a row of hams, ready for the summer rush. On the first night, I was awakened by a clawing and grunting noise, almost in my ear, and learned that a row of black bears spent each night on the outside of the clapboard wall sniffing the hams and clawing the thin splintered boards.

As the days passed the work crew increased until we were feeding nearly sixty men. I complained repeatedly to Sandy, the big boss from Mammoth

Hot Springs, whenever he dropped in. His only reply was to refer to the hundreds of unemployed lined up at Mammoth who would be glad to take the job. Then Ed and I worked up a plan for his next visit. We had been serving the men at tables of four and found this quite a burden. So, we pushed the tables into lines to make a couple of long tables, telling Sandy we could serve quicker this way. We put the food into a few serving dishes and let the hungry carpenters go to it. In a few moments, the tables were a tangle of arms and hands grabbing for food and slopping half of it over—"Just one big hog trough," as Sandy complained later. But he got the point and sent us two helpers the next day.

Our workload therefore eased somewhat and we finally had a chance to look around. The cafeteria faced Yellowstone Lake, a deep, clear sheet of blue water stretching fifteen miles to the south, rimmed by mountain ranges. Even in early June deep snowbanks remained in the bordering woods and the lake water never warmed up to the point of swimming comfort. Ed and I kept trying, but no matter how hot the sun, the water would turn us blue and chattering in about ninety seconds.

The lake's outlet, the crystal green Yellowstone River, flowed off to the north a short distance away. A wooden bridge, lined by fishermen in mid-season, crossed the outlet stream and gave its name to our cafeteria. The chief fringe benefit of my job was the free use of a rowboat at the Fishing Bridge boat dock. This perquisite of office became the main reason for my staying on the job.

Sometimes after supper we would row upstream against the swift current a hundred yards into the lake, and when the south wind blew we would try our skill against the five-foot combers. The boats were made of sheet metal, about twelve feet long, and handled well. Sometimes we would dodge rocks while floating downstream a mile or so through woodland and mountain meadow, but it was a job to row the boat back to the dock. All of this whetted my desire for the river cruise I had planned, but the long drop of Yellowstone Falls a few miles downstream and the heavy canyon rapids below meant that I would have to bypass a long stretch of the river to begin my trip.

On June 15 the summer help arrived at the park entrances in long trains of Pullman cars from Los Angeles and St. Paul. These were the "savages" who manned the hotels and cafeterias—college boys and girls, or teachers who had been up for many seasons. Along with the novices came a few experienced cooks and waitresses, the latter the hard-boiled kind who shouted the jargon of their trade in gravelly voices back to the kitchen: "stack" for an order of hotcakes, "drop two" for poached eggs, and "Adam and Eve on a raft" for poached eggs on toast.

Billy did not take kindly to the new regime. For some days, he had not spoken to Ed and went through the motions of firing him daily. "I know dem Irish tricks," he would mutter when he detected some minor lapse. He fired me just as often but I could kid him along with my college German and he used me as a go-between with the rest of the crew. But the savages were too much for him. He quit a few days later, shouting, "Gott tam—de womans haff drive me bughouse!"

Although my own situation was agreeable enough, in a few more weeks the urge to be on my way became overwhelming. Before building my boat at Livingston to run the lower river, I decided to explore Yellowstone Lake while I had the chance and therefore arranged to use one of the rowboats for a solo cruise.

With my camping outfit aboard I left the dock one windy evening, headed into the lake, and skirted the shore to row eastward. Just before sunset I landed in a sandy cove behind Storm Point, a promontory four miles east of Fishing Bridge. The waves dashed into water-worn caves at the cliff's base, causing a constant growling sound. I built a driftwood fire, dried out my clothes after a good meal, and rolled into my blanket on the clean white sand.

Friday, July 18, dawned under a hot, windless sky that foretold a day of storms. I rowed several miles across Mary Bay to Steamboat Point, where fumaroles sent steam clouds high in the air. Then I continued five miles to the south, along the east shore, to a cabin of the National Marine Fisheries Service. My next landing was planned for Park Point, at the entrance of the Southeast Arm. But the wind rose against me and I had a stiff pull towards the point. In leaving Fishing Bridge I had rigged the boat with a short mast and yard to carry a crude square sail made from a discarded awning. The furled sail added greatly to the wind resistance and I barely made shore before the storm arrived in crashing fury. Fortunately, there was a log cabin on the headland, where I weathered the storm under the porch and cooked lunch on my canned heat burner.

I embarked once more when the sun broke through, intending to sail out into the lake and spend the night on Frank Island. But I was hardly well started under canvas when another storm blew up from nowhere. Lightning bolts began striking the calm lake surface about a mile away, and then each succeeding bolt seemed to strike closer to me. When a bolt struck the lake surface there was no visible disturbance in the water, but the lightning dissipated in a horizontal sheet of fire over the glassy water. Not wishing to conduct an experiment in high-voltage electricity with this combination of a thunderstorm, a lake of ice water three hundred feet deep, and a metal rowboat, I turned and headed along the eastern shore.

A strong blast of wind now came up from the southeast, astern of my new course. A sudden gust parted both pieces of twine that I was using as sheets to hold the lower corners of the square sail. The unrestrained canvas now flapped furiously against the mast, threatening to snap it. Great whitecaps mounted astern and promised serious trouble if I should let her get broadside into the trough of the waves. Since the boat had no rudder, I was steering her from the stern with an oar when under sail. But I took a chance, dropped the oar, went forward for a few moments, and lashed the flapping canvas to the yard.

Then with the wind at full gale force behind me, I let her scud under the bare pole, keeping her head off the rocky shore by steering to the left with the oar. Wind pressure on the furled sail gave her steerage way and kept her head downwind, out of the trough of the waves. But the thought of my furled canvas graveled me so much that I decided to try her out under full sail at any cost. Off a shallow point the waves crested and broke into a smother of foam, giving me a chance to anchor in the shallows and unfurl the canvas. When the twine was replaced and the sail sheeted home I took in the anchor and the boat swung around before the gale like a bird on the wing.

Out of the shallows again, she leaped along under the pull of her little patch of canvas, hissing through the foam with incredible speed. Great foaming crests of grey-green water rose above her stern in menace, but just in time she would lift her square stern to avoid being swamped. Occasionally she would ride the crest like a surfboard, speeding along for ten or fifteen seconds until the wave outran her. These were the crucial moments— if I had let her swing around broadside to the breakers she would have rolled under like a barrel.

Once started on this ride there was no withdrawal; stolen glances at the rocky coast, white and misty behind the pounding breakers, told me I would find no safety there. Mossy cliffs and wooded banks flew past a few yards to the right. Soon the point near the fisheries cabin appeared ahead. Its shoal waters extended across my course, forming a welter of surf. Taking a chance on the depth, I shot directly across the white water on the shoal and surfboarded all the way. One breaker after another lifted her skyward and tobogganed her along. And then she was through, into the swells of the shallow bay. Soaking wet and shivering, I tied up at the dock and cooked a warm meal of rice and onions inside the cabin.

An hour later my clothes had dried and the gale had moderated to a strong, steady southeast wind. In late afternoon, I sailed beyond the point once more. The heaving waves looked like a millrace when I left the shelter of the bay, but the boat rode them well. I left Steamboat Point a mile to starboard and steered for the sandy cove behind Storm Point. The sail drew well and it was a pleasant voyage, with a bubbling wake to smooth the breakers when they surged high on the stern. At sundown, the water east towards the Absaroka Mountains was a wild sight; black racing waves, tinted red and green at their tumbling crests, moved across a panorama of glowering peaks and fiery sky. When darkness came my best pilot aid was the growling sea cave on Storm Point, now roaring and spitting froth from its jagged teeth. Soon the black bulk of Storm Point cut off the western sky and it was time to douse the canvas.

This exhilarating day of freshwater square sailing compensated for lack of the real thing. As I wrote my parents, "I think I learned more real seamanship from that lake cruise than from all last winter."

A few days later I collected my summer wages of $71.69 and shuffled down the highway to the park entrance in Gardiner, Montana. But my luck on the highway had vanished; most of the cars were loaded with camping gear and there wasn't a chance of a ride. With all of that cash in my pocket it would have been a small matter to buy a rail ticket to Livingston, but the hobo code prevailed and I decided to beat my way.

At the terminal in Gardiner a track workman, or "gandy dancer," told me that a tourist train would pull out soon and that I wouldn't have any trouble riding "blind baggage" down to Livingston. I hopped aboard as she was making up in the yards. The blind baggage door was the forward door of the baggage car, which was hooked on directly behind the locomotive tender. This door was kept locked, and the open vestibule around it made a sheltered place for hoboes to stand out of sight of the train crew. Here was the third rung in my climb up the ladder of the hoboing profession—or my descent into vagrancy, if you will. First, I had started hitchhiking down the Oregon highway, then I had hopped a freight on the Southern Pacific across the Nevada desert, and now I was catching a ride on a passenger train on the Northern Pacific.

The train hooked on more coaches in the yards and then loaded her passengers at the station. I slunk back into the folds of the accordion-like vestibule canvas, but no one bothered me and soon we were underway. The train rattled, the wheels screeched on the sharp canyon curves, and the soot rained on my face. Soon we were following the Yellowstone River in Yankee Jim Canyon, where I could see the heavy rapids that Lewis R. Freeman had described in *Down the Yellowstone*. Sixty miles from Gardiner the train rolled into Livingston station and I jumped off during a thunderstorm.

I felt right at home in a river town like Livingston. First, I walked down to the river to look it over and was not disappointed in what I found: the Yellowstone was a lively stream whose green waters coursed over a bed of gravel and boulders through constant riffles and some rapids.

Next I called on the Hornbecks and was invited to use their garden house for my lodgings. Then I stopped by the A. W. Miles Lumber and Coal Company, where the manager agreed to let me work in the carpentry shop and use their tools if I would buy my lumber there. Finally, inevitably, I gravitated to the quiet little public library to pass the rest of the day and to consult my pilot guide for the river trip: Lewis R. Freeman's book.

The next morning, Saturday, July 26, I started work at the lumberyard. Sharing the shop with me was a young Viking, just over from Norway, who helped design my craft by sketching the boats he had used in the highlands of his home country, which are skidded over the mountain meadows from one lake to another. My carpentry was strictly of the mountain-cabin class and I had no intention of putting a curve in any part of the boat. It was to be a square-ended punt—strictly a packing case type of job. I had figured on an overall length of fourteen feet, but when I actually saw the long boards I quickly changed my mind. I bought ten-foot boards of 1" x 8" no. 3 Western fir—a cheap grade, but the knotholes could always be caulked. I spent the morning building up the two sides of the scow by cleating two of the 8" boards together to make sides 16" high. I trimmed them to fit the slope of the bow and stern and then discovered that I had cleated them both alike, not allowing for the fact that they would go on opposite sides. In the afternoon I undid this error and got as far as planking her bow and stern, using a heavy tar compound to caulk the seams.

On Monday I put in eleven hours at the shop and had a boat by the time I quit. I planked her bottom, nailed on three reinforcing planks as fore-and-aft skids to slide her over rocks, planked over her bow for three feet as a splash deck, and made a thwart and mast step. At this stage I had some vague plan of sailing her when the wind was right, and figured on using her sail as a tent in case of rain. I put on a splash coaming, fitted a grating in the bottom, and painted her a dark green on the outside and grey inside. Oars were not to be bought in Livingston so I made a crude pair by ripping a 2x4 down the middle and tacking a paddle-shaped board on the ends.

Word soon got around about my trip. Several old-timers—trappers and others who had used the river for downhill transportation in the old days—came by to spin a yarn about the terrors of the Yellowstone rapids. They did not think much of my handiwork and there was some shaking of heads about her coffin-like appearance. Word also got to the *Livingston Enterprise*. I did not enjoy the suicidal implication of the newspaper headline: "TIRED OF HITCH-HIKING HE WILL TRY THE RIVER!"

I learned of many river tragedies. It was easy to tell that the Yellowstone would be a raging torrent each spring when the snowfields melted on the Continental Divide, and that even a strong swimmer would have a hard time in continuous rapids and icy water. Many signs pointed to higher water stages: barked and bent willow shoots clinging to gravel bars, fields of boulders deposited by a mighty current, and driftwood caught in pockets high above the normal river level. I happened to hit the Yellowstone at the very beginning of the big drought of the 1930s that was to have such a tragic impact on the West. I was able to ride a fairly good flow of water, but it would be a long time between blizzards and rainstorms for several years to come.

One afternoon I paid my bill of $8.35 at the lumberyard and had the gleaming scow hauled down to the river at the 9th Street bridge. When I launched her in the main channel I was appalled to see water spurting in through the carefully tarred seams. In an hour or so she swelled up nicely, however, and when I dumped the water out her seams held fairly well. I rowed down past an island and was hailed by a couple of kids from shore. I picked them up for a short ride, but dropped them above a stretch of whitewater. Johnny Marquette, age nine, and his friend became an appreciative gallery for my descent of the foaming riffle. I tied her up for the night in a bank of nettles and the next day caulked a few leaks in her tarred seam.

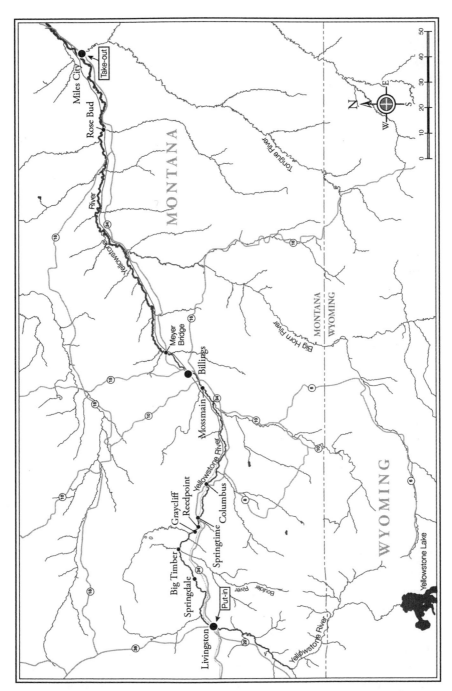

A map of the Yellowstone River showing the stretch from Livingston to Miles City, Montana, run by Harold Leich. Although this map shows the locations of some current roads and highways, these were not all built at the time Leich made his trip. Map by Thomas Child.

SATURDAY, AUGUST 2, was the date of my departure. The Hornbecks and their friends as well as Johnny and his mother were there to see me off. I left the Harvat Bridge at 9:30, rowing briskly to demonstrate the boat to the assemblage. On the fifth stroke the port rowlock wrenched loose and nearly spilled me into the stream. Fortunately the current soon carried me around a bend to the accompaniment of mutual arm-waving.

And now I was off on the long-planned voyage. Sitting on the stern thwart and trying to steer with a six-foot sweep, I let her ride in the swift current. Quickly the neat houses of Livingston dropped astern and a panorama of woods and mountains slipped by on either side. My camping gear and food were stowed in the packsack under the splash deck, I had a tarpaulin in case of storms, and not a care faced me. This was hoboing deluxe, catching a ride on the clear green current amidst some of the finest scenery in America. What a princely way to head back home! As long as the boat stayed afloat I would be self-sufficient; like the shanty-boaters of the Ohio I could lead a vagrant Huck Finn life.

But the Yellowstone is no place to daydream, as I discovered when I tried to avoid a shoal by steering with the sweep. Since the punt was drifting with the current she had no forward speed and therefore would not respond to her helm. She banged to a stop on the shoal gravel bottom. Then the sweep came into its true use: as a pole to shove her into deeper water. I finally stopped using it in favor of rowing downstream to work up some steerage way and found that with the oars I could easily spin the boat around to miss rocks or shoals. This was a great improvement in technique, at the cost of a stiff neck from peering over my shoulder at the hazards ahead.

Stretches of whitewater were frequent, separated by slower reaches of the river. Below the railroad bridge at Livingston I entered a sharp riffle under a rocky cape. The scow slapped nicely over the curling waves but occasionally plunged her stubby nose under a breaker and doused me with foam. Several miles on I rounded a sharp bend above another railroad bridge. Too late I realized that a large lump of water ahead concealed a boulder dangerously near the surface. I was glad of her reinforced bottom when she crashed on the rock. Next she swung broadside into a great overlapping breaker in a depression below the boulder. Somehow she plunged through without my having a thing to do with it. Before I could dip an oar she rode into smooth water under the bridge; I was merely a passenger in a runaway boat. Clearly I had some lessons to learn on "reading the water."

Soon the canyon above Springdale opened ahead and I could hear the mutter of whitewater. Since the old timers had warned me this was one of the worst stretches, I entered the gorge's narrowing walls with some alarm. The first section I found easy going, but lower down came a bit of whitewater that gave her a real test. She weaved through it nicely, only shipping one wave over her bow. I was pleased at her performance in the first real test she had met.

When I landed for lunch I had a chance to study the play of the surges. This had ceased to be a poetic exercise in the beauty of swift water and was becoming a lesson in survival. I noticed that river waves are quite different from those raised on quiet water by the wind. Big green waves rolled upstream at the exact speed of the current and thus stayed in the same place in relation to the shore. Though of different origin, they reminded me of the string of high waves tailing out behind an Ohio River sternwheeler. These standing waves ("haystacks" to a river runner) sometimes reared themselves into translucent crests that broke in a smother of white and then collapsed for a few moments before breaking again. This tumbling dance of the breakers in a savage river rapid struck me as one of the most fascinating sights in nature.

The haystacks occurred in series of eight or more big foaming waves, where the swift current was constricted by ledges jutting out from the banks, or where the riverbed dropped. The head of the rapid was often marked by a "V" with its point downstream. The "V"—or tongue—was glassy smooth but broke into haystacks where the sides narrowed into the point. I learned that it was usually best to sail right down the middle of the tongue to avoid the constricting ledges on either side.

At the tail of a rapid the haystacks would dwindle until there was just a path of swift water knifing between two pools of slower water. Sometimes whirlpools played along the dividing line and if I got the boat partly into slow water she would cant and spin alarmingly.

Below Springdale, in the early afternoon, I noticed a black thundercloud astern, rapidly eating up the blue Montana sky. A strong headwind sprang up, right into the swiftly approaching storm. Then came the real blow from the opposite direction: rain drove in sheets and wind lashed up white foam on the river. The punt scudded before it, all my efforts to control her course proving useless. She struck on a boulder, swung broadside, and threatened to capsize under the weight of wind, wave, and current. But fast work, using the sweep as a pole, cleared her in time and she ran before the storm again.

Towards evening the sky cleared to the west and the low rays of the sun brightened the green of the rain-drenched willows. Great blue herons soared from sunlit treetops or perched on swaying branches like pterodactyls. A flock of ducks that I had chased all afternoon beat the water white and rose in formation. A double rainbow shone against the black storm cloud, now disappearing to the east over the white houses and red grain elevators of Big Timber, Montana. Far behind on the horizon a jagged range pierced a golden band of clouds, the peaks looming blue against the clear western sky.

The rapids at Big Timber, bad according to my informants, proved to be nothing but tiny ripples. I continued past town and camped in the cottonwoods near the mouth of the Boulder River, thirty-three miles from Livingston by road and more by water. Thoroughly pleased with the day's adventures, I dried out by the campfire, cooked a hot dinner, and turned in early. It rained during the night and I was glad to have the canvas cover over my blanket. It also gave me some protection from swarms of hungry mosquitoes. I loafed around camp until 11:30 the next morning, drying out my spare clothes that had become soaked even though they were in the packsack.

The Boulder River was running high and yellow with mud as I passed the next morning, showing that the rainstorm had concentrated in its valley. For a mile below its mouth there was a line between its yellow waters and the green Yellowstone. Then the waters slowly merged, the mud an easy victor.

I got into a sharp riffle above Greycliff. In the middle of it rose a three-foot haystack, nearly perpendicular. "She'll go now, if ever," I told myself, but the punt rose to it superbly with her bluff bow. At noon I was drifting idly along a broad reach with a high bank along one side. Suddenly a crash like thunder sounded ahead. I turned to see that a wide section of the twenty-foot-high clay and gravel bank had collapsed into the river. A compact dust cloud hung below the cliff for some moments and then vanished in the wind. A boat caught under that weight of earth would have vanished completely.

When I tied up at Greycliff for supplies a man told me the river was smooth sailing to Reedpoint, twelve miles below. I hadn't gone a mile, however, when I barged into the worst rapids yet. Two successive breakers nearly swamped her. She climbed over the first wave well enough, but then wham!—down into the next one, buried in foam. As she lifted her nose, gallons of yellow water cascaded over the deck coaming into the cockpit. Six inches of water sloshed around until I bailed it out with my hat. None of my consultants in Livingston had mentioned the place, and I was rapidly losing confidence in their advice.

Actually, the forces of erosion constantly change a river's character; you should not blindly follow any river guide. Spring floods will sweep away bars, boulders, and tree trunks from one spot and build up new obstructions in another. A few catastrophic storms in a century will bring down landslides that may create new rapids. Bedrock ledges, of course, do not change noticeably in one man's lifetime, but the rapids they cause may change greatly according to the river stage. Some may run worse at low water and be tamely submerged in a flood. Others may become much more turbulent and dangerous at high water.

During the day I ran some cross-riffles, where two opposing currents were sent off by ledges on opposite sides of the river, mostly in narrow gorges. Where they met in the center there would be a nasty chop, and often sidewinding waves would lick along the boat's sides and climb aboard. My boat did some real pitching and rolling in those places.

Sometimes it is hard to distinguish between a riffle and a rapid. A riffle is a swift place in the current—usually caused by a shallow gravel bar—where the surface is ruffled into wavelets or even waves two or three feet high. A true rapid is more savage and is usually caused by bedrock ledges or large boulders over which the river roars in great waves and whirlpools.

In the afternoon I passed extensive beaver cuttings along the banks; the animals had evidently come back strong since the middle of the nineteenth century when the mountain men (trappers who preceded the settlers) had nearly cleaned them out. It was pleasant going the rest of the way to Reedpoint, and a flock of turkeys roosting on a fence rail welcomed me with assorted gobbles. I camped in a sheep pasture a mile below town and fixed a fine supper of roasted corn, spaghetti, and canned pears.

The next day, August 4, brought the climax of my river trip. I got up just after dawn, breakfasted on pears and grapenuts, and shoved into the current. Some miles below Springtime I entered the strongest rapids I had run so far. I had been experimenting with rowing techniques and now had a chance to try something new. Instead of rowing downstream, craning my neck to have a look ahead, I swung the boat around and let her drift down stern first, poised at the oars to row upstream in the current in order to control her course.

This had several advantages. I obviously had a better view of the river ahead. Also, I could steer better when I rowed against the current since this gave the boat more time to crab across the stream into the best position. More important, her bow eased into the breaking waves at a speed slower than the current instead of smashing into them at a speed faster than the current. Thus, she could weather rougher seas than with the old head-on attack. If the current was not too swift I could even poise on the tongue of a rapid for a few moments until I chose the best course to follow. Unknowingly, by trial and error I had evolved into using the same whitewater technique that had been used for many years in Canada and in the heavy cataracts of the Colorado River canyons.

These rapids, a long series of high foaming waves, ran in a branch of the stream beneath a high pine-clad cliff on the right bank. As I rowed slowly against the current the boat's bow rose easily to the combers. They were of such power that I would have been swamped with my previous technique. She tossed up and down and rolled back and forth with crashing yellow breakers all around. This was the spell of swift water: to ride the combers in a little ten-foot crate hardly bigger than the packing case we had rowed on Bee Slough and to feel the mastery of placing her exactly where I wanted to. She came through with the deck almost dry.

I landed for groceries at Columbus before lunch and inquired fruitlessly about Stillwater Rapids, supposed to be the strongest below Livingston (despite the name). Four miles below town were two short rapids, both creaming with steep, treacherous waves. The boat made them both without shipping a drop.

But then came the best fun. The boat entered a quarter-mile stretch of the fastest, roughest water yet, curving to the left through a canyon with a steep wall on the right. The waves were longer and higher than I had seen before and they foamed at their curling crests. It was great while it lasted, weaving in and out, her bow shooting skyward and then plunging into the trough. She rose nicely to the worst of them when I held her back with the oars.

Further down high, overhanging cliffs projected over the river. The boat sailed right under the arched, rocky roof, which was plastered with the mud nests of cliff swallows. Then a small branch followed the cliff's base to the right, while the main stream continued ahead. I entered this inviting side canyon without hesitation. As the gorge narrowed the current quickened. For fifty yards the current went down straight, breaking into long, smooth waves. Then came a sharp curve to the right, around a jutting, overhanging cliff. And there at the corner was the highest crest of all, leaving me barely enough headroom to slip beneath the stony portcullis. Up and down she went, with a long dip and a slow roll. I ducked for an instant and then she was riding smoothly down an open valley.

That was the last of the whitewater, but the fine scenery continued, with great cliffs and palisades marching down the right bank. Instead of riffles and rapids I encountered shoals where the current slowed down and spring floods had deposited gravel bars. As in a river delta, the stream divided and then subdivided into a network of small braided channels. It was tricky to guess which one continued all the way through—the smaller ones just disappeared when their waters percolated into the gravel bed and dried up. I tried to pick the largest channels, but once I wound up high and dry on the gravel while the main stream, collecting itself out of the seeping gravel banks, rolled by several yards away and a good three feet lower. It was a job to skid the boat down to the water so I could resume my free ride.

In the evening I bought some milk and eggs at a riverside ranch and camped a short distance below, near Mossmain. According to the roadmap I had rowed and drifted sixty miles, a day never to be forgotten.

It was slow going the next morning to Billings and a long, hot walk into town, but I was rewarded with seven letters at the post office (via general delivery). After two mild rapids below town the going became hot and dull. I was emerging from the rimrock palisades of the upper river into a broad valley where the river gradient became almost imperceptible. The whole situation flattened out. Instead of a clear stream dashing down between colorful cliffs with pines and cedars scattered along the ledges, I was riding a sluggish current between low shores of eroding mud.

Drinking water became a problem. I had been able to fill my glass jug at ranch houses along the way, but the drought had struck the lower valley. One ranch had none to spare and another one provided water that I could not swallow because of a strong alkaline taste. Finally I got some that was drinkable, although it had flakes of a white mineral swirling around in it.

The next day was the same—hot sun, frequent shoals, and long dead stretches. The only relief was to strip and swim a while, pushing the boat along to make some progress. I kept on rowing after sunset, under a bright moon, and enjoyed the cool evening. Myriad squeaking bats hovered near the boat and defended me from mosquitoes. Suddenly the night erupted into loud squawks when I disturbed a great blue heron. He soared above the boat in wide circles, from the Big Dipper to Cassiopeia and back again. Then two sections of the North Coast Limited, a crack passenger train, roared by on the Northern Pacific tracks that skirted the bank. Finally I camped near Meyer Bridge.

The following day brought no improvement; after a hot day of rowing I continued by moonlight and camped below Forsyth. Friday was distinguished by an encounter with a bulldog when I asked for water at a ranch house—my trousers and ankle lost. In the town of Rosebud I had a long talk with the village druggist, who gave me some pulp magazines, newspapers, and orange pop. I drifted in the afternoon heat with my hat pulled down against the sun, reading *Astounding Stories*. Reviving after sunset, I rowed for several moonlit hours.

On Saturday, August 9, I rowed all morning in the sluggish current and reached Miles City at noon. Here my river trip ended, 266 miles from Livingston by road and many more by the river's meanders. The next morning I sold the punt to a farmer for $1.50. He needed some wood for a hencoop—a sad fate indeed for a whitewater craft. I decided to head for home and shambled over to the hobo jungle near the Northern Pacific yards. As the *Livingston Enterprise* would have said, "TIRED OF THE RIVER HE WILL RIDE THE RAILS!"

Many years later recollections of my river trip came back during long night watches on the Pacific Ocean:

"To the Yellowstone"—1930

Green in the sunlight your waters were leaping
And white was the crest of each tumbling wave;
River of youth, in the strength of my morning
What wild exultation your swift current gave!

The sky of Montana arose like an archway
From rimrock to rimrock in sparkling blue.

Down through the canyons of yellow and scarlet
I rode through your rapids with song and halloo.

River of morning, swift son of the mountains,
Your snow-melted waters must flow to the sea
Mingled with silt and the sewage of cities
Where vast sluggish currents engulf you, once free.

Waters of crystal that surged in the sunlight,
We measured our moment for ecstasy's fee;
How can we grieve then the fates that befall us
As we flow through the lowlands to go to the sea?[2]

CHAPTER TWO

Bewitched

T HE STORY OF MY TRAVELS was a one-day wonder to my family and friends and then it was time to settle down to a respectable life. In the fall of 1930, Evansville—like the rest of the nation—was caught in an economic whirlpool and could barely keep afloat. I dabbled in life insurance and worked in the family business, but gradually became dissatisfied and reverted to the seat of all my troubles: the public library. Sometimes I dropped in to browse when I should have been calling on insurance prospects. One fateful day a new title caught my eye: *Down the World's Most Dangerous River*, by an author with the fluvial name of Clyde Eddy.[1] I sat right down and read the book in a couple of hours and knew when I finished that someday I would try the heavy rapids of the Colorado canyons.

In the spring of 1931 I was offered a summer job back in the White Mountains, building two new huts for the Appalachian Mountain Club. This release to the outdoors from the routines of business could not be resisted, and I left on May 15, riding the company truck as far as Terre Haute. Various rides on the highway and a ticket on an interurban line got me to Anderson, Indiana, about 5:30 p.m. The Knickerbocker Express, a crack passenger flyer from St. Louis to New York, was due at 5:54 p.m. I just had time to walk over to the Big Four Station when she rolled in from the west.

I boarded her tender across from the station, hung alongside on the iron ladder until she started, and then climbed on top of the water tank behind the coal pile. This wide, flat deck was far better than the blind baggage door. It was a fine ride at sunset, roaring across the flatlands of Indiana and Ohio in the cool evening. We changed train crews at Bellefontaine and took the last lap to Cleveland with only one stop for water.

She pulled into the yards at Lyndale after dark, in a glare of arc lights. The firemen had warned me to unload because they would hook on an electric locomotive to take her into the Cleveland passenger station. When I jumped off I saw a harness bull walking towards the train from a string of freight cars. He didn't see me right away, giving me a chance to break for some boxcars farther up the line. Then he started in pursuit; it was hide and seek for a few minutes among the shadows and the cars until I lost him. I climbed a car ladder for a few minutes so he couldn't see my legs on the ground and then broke across the tracks for open country, out of the lighted yard.

A bus took me into Cleveland, and there I caught a streetcar out to Collinwood, on the east side of town, where the steam locomotives were hooked on again. These yards, too, were flooded by arc lights so there was no chance to catch a ride on a passenger locomotive undetected. I found an empty boxcar and went to sleep, a long haul from Evansville in one day.

The next morning I hopped a freight train headed east and found a comfortable nook in a loaded coal gondola. In one corner the coal did not quite fill the car to the brim, leaving a cozy spot where I curled up, using my pack as a pillow. After a long sleep it seemed to me that things had become mighty quiet. I peered over the edge and found that my gondola was standing alone on a sidetrack out in the open country, near a deserted factory. A ride on the highway brought me to Conneaut, a pleasant town near the Pennsylvania line. Here I washed my face, had a good lunch of lake pike, and loafed near the passenger station waiting for something to happen.

Nothing was stirring on the New York Central, but the Nickel Plate tracks a few yards away offered more promise. A hotshot freight highballed in the yards and started to roll. Five or six of us ran alongside, but she must have been doing twenty miles an hour by then and most of us didn't make it. Then I fell in with a middle-aged hobo who had once had the entire side of his face smashed in, leaving an awful scar. We quickly formed one of those unspoken partnerships of the road that can last for an hour or a week. We talked to a friendly switchman and learned that a second hotshot would leave in a few minutes. Scarface and I caught her on the fly about 5 p.m. and found ourselves on a flatcar loaded with a huge piece of machinery, a cross between a harvester and a ditchdigger. Its hood offered shelter when it started to rain, but at the first stop Scarface found an empty boxcar and we shifted our flag. We slept in comfort to Buffalo while it rained furiously outside.

Hoboes had no fear of the train crews themselves; with the increasing number of free riders in the depression the crews could not show much hostility, whatever their true feelings. Thus hoboes no longer had to ride under the cars on rods or other dangerous perches. They rode openly in empty boxcars, known as side-door Pullmans, or in gondolas, flatcars, or reefers. The various railroad detectives, or bulls, were thoroughly discussed and estimates made of their various degrees of hostility. Gruesome stories were told about what the bulls had done to a hobo or what a gang of hoboes had done to a bull. "Hostile" (pronounced with a hard "i") was the most frequently used adjective in the conversation.

In the vivid talk of the hobo, anyone not on the road himself or connected with the railroad or the police was known as a home guard: a simple soul who stayed home and did not share in the adventurous world we knew.

It was late evening when we unloaded. The neon lights of town, glaring from skyscrapers far beyond the shimmering rails of steel, glistened in grim reflection off the shattered face of my partner. We crossed an iron bridge over the oily depths of a small river and walked up the walled confines of the yard until arc lights ahead signaled the danger zone. We found a telegraph pole fitted with climbing spikes near the embankment and a short scramble brought us to the street.

Scarface slunk up to a group on a pool-room corner and asked the way to the other end of the yards. One of them turned to me and said, "Which way you headin', Slim?"

"East."

"That's easy. Grab a blind at the Central Terminal," and he pointed to the New York Grand Central Terminal building in the distance, a massive tower bathed in floodlights.

"Never did like them passenger trains," Scarface muttered and wandered off to find himself a flop for the night. I continued along a wide boulevard that headed for the station. In fact, the boulevard was swallowed by the station, ending in a turning circle inside the building. I walked across the brightly lighted area, stared back at a few late travelers who glared at me, and gained the shadow beyond the building.

Here was a region of winking red and green lights—a sea of glinting rails. Dark figures passed silently along a narrow dirt runway. A huge rushing shape roared by with a blinding glare of a headlight and slowed with a screech of airbrakes. Down the path from the roundhouse came a railroad man swinging a lunch bucket. When I asked him if there was anything headed east he replied, "The Limited's over there on track twenty-five getting ready to pull out." A sweep of his lunch bucket showed her taking on passengers and mail under the station sheds.

The Limited! He meant, of course, the Twentieth Century Limited or the Southwestern Limited, the finest trains in America and the peak of the hoboing profession. In addition to the usual dining, club, and observation cars they provided shower baths, a barber shop, and a public stenographer (I could have used a shower bath about that time). The Twentieth Century Limited ran from Chicago to New York and its running mate, the Southwestern Limited, ran from St. Louis to Boston. The eastbound sections would both be due in Buffalo sometime around midnight or so.

Whatever her name, there she stood, hissing and steaming, clanging and panting. A host of people milled along her sides—passengers and spectators, porters and conductors, mail clerks and redcaps. Above them all the engineer sat aloof, leaning from his cab window to catch the conductor's highball signal.

In approaching her I swung way around ahead of the big Hudson-type steam locomotive to avoid the lighted passenger platform. Then I was safe, on the opposite side of the train, hidden in darkness. Slowly, swathed in steam, I crept past pistons, drive wheels, and the firebox and on to the blind baggage vestibule. I scrambled up into the vestibule behind the tender, glanced around, and jumped for the iron ladder on the tender. Once on top, I threw myself flat on the level deck of the water tank and wriggled out of the packsack to avoid disclosure.

In the few minutes before she highballed I spread-eagled across the iron deck while my clothing soaked up pools of oily water and ground into layers of coal dust. Then she was pulling out and the end of the train shed slowly slipped past my nose. I crawled to the edge and looked down at the blind baggage door. Safe—not a soul in sight. The receding clock on the Grand Central Terminal tower showed one minute past midnight. A vision of Scarface swept my mind: Scarface out on the lonely streets trying to stem a cup of coffee and a flop. Well, I wouldn't need a flop that night.

As the train gathered speed in the yards, I groped in the packsack and found my shabby leather jacket and some dungarees. Bracing myself against a raised hatch on the water tank, I slipped them on for added warmth. Already the cold wind was curling around the tender in bitter gusts.

Out in the open country she began to ramble. Once, as she swung around a curve at high speed, I was thrown from the hatch cover and sprawled to the edge, but one hand caught a low guardrail and steadied me. After that I squatted on the cover and clung to the under edge. Even though I was riding backwards, a stream of cinders beat into my face and a steam exhaust swirled vapor into my eyes whenever I half-opened them.

About half an hour after leaving the station, as she roared along a straightaway, I suddenly felt the iron hatch cover begin to slam up and down beneath me. Water began to gush from all sides of the hatch, pouring out by the barrel, soaking my legs and my body before it cascaded over the side. Then I remembered: the fellows had told me about the crack trains on the New York Central Railroad—how they took water on the fly by scooping it up from a long trough between the rails. This was the overflow from the water tank beneath me, forcing its way out of the manhole and lifting the heavy hinged cover I was using for a seat.

I perched on the cover again when the overflow stopped. A wave of dirty water sloshed across the deck when the tender leaned on the curves. Soon we were tearing through Rochester at seventy miles an hour. Then we pulled up inside a cavernous building. The fireman scrambled over the high ridge of coal on the tender, shouted an order to some men on a scaffold beside the train, and guided the descending coal chute. As it approached he jumped aboard a small shelf and rode along the tender while ton after ton of coal rumbled out of the chute. I had risen to watch this spectacle but flattened out in a hurry when the conductor strolled nearby.

Once more we were roaring across the open countryside under the winking lights of the Big Dipper, which was partially obscured by a long trail of smoke and steam that raced close by over my head. I crouched on the cold iron hatch of the water tank, shivering in my wet clothes, and gradually lost all reckoning of time or place. I was part of a mad rushing comet that shot across the paths of stars with a long white streamer in its trail. The only light came from those stars that we had just missed and from the long ghostly banner in our wake. I was the comet—streaking through the night across the paths of stars. . . .

The bouncing hatch and a douche of cold water in the right place revived me soon enough. The fireman had told me to ride on top of the coal pile if

I wanted to keep dry. I tried it for a while but somehow it didn't seem so good—too much wind and flying coal dust. Also there was nothing to hang onto—you just had to spread-eagle on the lumps of coal, keeping on the very top of the high ridge because the sides sloped down to, well, nothing.

And then, when we whizzed under a low bridge, a disturbing thought came to me. I looked ahead at the smokestack and looked around behind me. Sure enough, I was the highest object on the whole train, perched on the coal pile waiting to be swept away if I raised up too high under the next bridge. I waited until the next time she took on water, saw it boil over the deck, and then carefully climbed down again to the water tank hatch. I got soaked once more before Syracuse and stretched out flat while she stopped in the main street.

From there we made the run to Albany without a break. She scooped up water occasionally and each time I sprawled to the low rail while water gushed from the manhole, filled the deck a foot deep, and sloshed over-board. I was soaked eight times altogether between Buffalo and Albany and sat and shivered in between.

A lovely dawn came as we roared down the Mohawk Valley past Little Falls and Amsterdam. We tore through Schenectady and a short time later ran down the hill in broad daylight into Albany. I cleared off as she rolled into the station and ran back along the embankment until I reached a stairway leading to the street. As I glanced back at the train I saw a familiar illuminated medallion on the railing of the observation car: "Southwestern Limited," the train I had ridden on my first trip to college and on the few occasions I returned home for vacations instead of skiing in the north country.

In a dirty hash house near the station I found that I could barely speak—my teeth were chattering so hard. I was eventually able to make something come out, and asked the proprietor if I could wash up. He was so startled that he didn't refuse. I scoured my face and hands with Old Dutch Cleanser and in half an hour was ready for a good breakfast.

The morning sun was warm along the Hudson. I found a secluded park near a deserted five-masted schooner where I stripped down, emptied my packsack, and had everything dry in an hour.

Around mid-morning I sauntered across the Hudson River Bridge with a hobo who told me the yard bulls on the Boston and Albany were hostile. He advised me to walk east for a mile or so along the tracks and catch the freights where they had to slow down on a grade. While waiting along the tracks as he suggested, I fell asleep in a pasture and woke up several hours later to find one side of my face badly sunburned. Finally I took a bus to Troy and then hit the highway, doing well all afternoon and reaching Rutland, Vermont, by nightfall, where I found a good room and had a bath.

The next day I repaid, at least symbolically, the kindness of the dozens of drivers who had helped me on the highways from Oregon to New England. I was riding with a man who had come all the way from New York City without sleep, along the slow roads of those days. As he drove down a steep hill into the White River Valley of Vermont he suddenly steered directly for the first post of a guardrail on the left side of the road, above a fifty-foot gully. I shot a glance at his face and saw that he was sound asleep. I grabbed the wheel with one hand just in time. He woke up with a start, was profuse in his thanks, and asked me to drive the rest of the way to White River Junction.

At the end of the summer some of us were sitting around a cherry red stove in a tent perched on a mountain ridge overlooking the Pemigewasset Wilderness. Our construction job on Galehead Hut had stopped because of the third day of rain, the supply of western thrillers had given out, and even poker was beginning to pale. Idly, I reached for a dirty newspaper under the flap of canvas that formed our door—somebody's copy of the *Lewiston Sun*. A small news item caught my eye:

> Syracuse, N.Y., Sept 4 (AP) The crushed bodies of two unidentified men were found on the tender of a westbound Twentieth Century Limited as it approached the New York Central station here tonight. The bodies were discovered by the fireman as the train slowed up. It was believed the men had been killed as the train sped under some bridge along the line.

The ragged sheet fluttered to the floor. My eyes seemed to pierce the canvas walls and capture a gleam of starlight from another universe while my mind caught the memory of a cold, roaring terror.

Back home that fall, in the depths of the Great Depression, I was fortunate to get my first really decent job since leaving college: as a field representative for the old Sunbeam Electric Manufacturing Company of Evansville. They were prospering by making refrigeration units for the new Coldspot home refrigerators sold by the expanding chain of Sears Roebuck retail stores. Several of us were hired to learn the business in the factory and then go out to train the Sears force in selling and repairing the new gadgets.

After spending the winter in the factory repairing old units on the salvage line, I went on the road in March 1932, riding the cushions this time. In Texas I went out "west of the Pecos" to repair refrigerators in the hot tin shacks of workers in the booming new oil fields, staying in square-fronted hotels in muddy little towns. When I returned home, my friends asked me how it felt to ride inside the train; actually it was much like the old hobo life, except for keeping clean and getting paid. Temporarily it satisfied my wish for travel.

Business conditions were still not improving in 1932. Hoboes were riding the freights in hundreds, as I could see from my Pullman window, and the stock market scraped bottom. In the summer of 1932 I walked across Boston Common one evening and estimated that five hundred men were sleeping out on newspapers.

There were plentiful reminders of my own days on the road. One evening I taxied to the Buffalo Central Terminal and rode a sleeper on the New York Central to Utica, less than a year after riding the tender of the Southwestern Limited over the same route. Our factory representative in New York took me to lunch at the Transportation Club, the rendezvous of railroad presidents, my erstwhile but unwitting benefactors. One day I caught a glimpse of the *Sea Thrush* in New York and later I boarded the *Wind Rush* in Bridgeport. The line had switched to Filipino crews so I learned little of my old shipmates.

The desperate winter of 1932–33 hit many companies that had held out until then. In a hotel room in Pittsburgh I could hear snatches of an evening sales meeting next door. There was little of the "inspirational pep talk" that one expects on such occasions and the big boss several times intoned, "Gentlemen, what is the end to be?"

Sunbeam, too, was having troubles. I was furloughed in November at Greenfield, Massachusetts, and hiked the snowy trails of the White Mountains once more, visiting my classmate Bob Monahan and other friends who were setting up a weather observatory on the frigid, wind-blown summit of Mount Washington. Back home I was lucky to get a blue-collar job repairing refrigerators on the Sunbeam salvage line. Business activity throughout the nation and the world hit bottom. But after the bank holiday in March things improved and we all cleaned our fingernails and fanned out to our territories again in the spring of 1933.

In the early 1930s the American steam locomotive reached the peak of its development, before the inroads of the diesel engine. Here was something as perfect of its kind as the great square-riggers I had longed to steer. As a professional traveling man I had a chance to both watch the show and get paid for it. Sometimes I was the only spectator; many an evening I rode out alone, the only passenger on a Pullman car. Most of the passengers seemed to be riding freights.

One morning I stood waiting at the New York Central passenger station at Westfield, New York, when a fast freight came by at sixty-five or seventy miles an hour. The ground trembled under her pounding drive wheels, the cinders flew, and dozens of dingbats on her flatcars held on through the steam and soot. One evening in the streets of Altoona I watched a long, loaded coal train come down the mountain from Horseshoe Curve in Pennsylvania. The brakes were set on the coal gondolas and she roared through town with sparks flying, axles smoking, and brakes screeching.

But this was not enough to overcome my restlessness and I felt the lack of challenge in the routine world of business. My thoughts kept returning to Clyde Eddy's adventures on the Colorado. In the public libraries along my route (including Boston, Springfield, Hartford, and many other cities), I read all I could find about the river: Major John Wesley Powell's account of his pioneering voyage through the Grand Canyon, Dellenbaugh's recollections as a member of Powell's second party,[2] Stone's book,[3] the Kolb brothers' magnificent story,[4] and many others. My old mentor of the Yellowstone, Lewis R. Freeman, helped me again with his two books about the Colorado River.[5]

Some years before, the U.S. Geological Survey had published contour maps of the Colorado from the mouth of the Green River to the Mexican border that showed every gulch and cataract. I bought a set and pored over them in hotel rooms from Ohio to Maine. Water Supply Paper 617, *Upper Colorado River and its Utilization* by Robert Follansbee, answered many of my questions about the headwaters.[6] If I were serious about the trip there was no time to lose. Work had already begun on Boulder Dam in Black Canyon (now Hoover Dam), and in a year or so its lake would back up and drown some of the best rapids in the Grand Canyon. After that no river trip could claim the full glory of the unspoiled canyon.

The very names on the maps began to work a spell: the Never Summer Range, Middle Park, Westwater Canyon, Mt. Tukuhnikivatz, Dead Horse

Point, the Dirty Devil River, the Land of Standing Rocks, and towns like Radium, Rifle, Antlers, and Moab. The cataracts of the Colorado, roaring in lonely canyons, had attracted the explorer, the trapper, the gold seeker, the scientist, and the sportsman long before my time, since the day when Alarcon, Coronado's lieutenant, discovered the great stream over four hundred years ago. Although notable expeditions had navigated the gorges of the Green River and thence down the Colorado through the Grand Canyon, a voyage starting on the Upper Colorado River and down to the Gulf of California had never been made.

Most of the successful voyages through the Grand Canyon had been well-financed and manned, using several boats to provide an ample safety margin. No one had ever done it single-handed. I decided to try it and to go alone. This would be a good way to launch my hoped-for career as a travel and adventure writer. As an experienced outdoorsman I fully recognized the risks that a single-handed voyage entailed, with no safety margin to allow for a wrecked boat or a broken leg. The truth of the matter is that I was drugged—bewitched—by a roaring golden river two thousand miles away that I had never even seen.

In May I bought a packsack and rain shirt in a Boston sporting goods store from Charlie Proctor, a college friend from the ski trails. At Abercrombie & Fitch's in New York I found a "gummikleiderbeutel" on sale, a large rubber clothing sack for canoeing, imported as a sample from Germany. I had bought a battered folding rubber kayak from a German in Cincinnati the year before. My decision was made and on May 30, 1933, I mailed in my resignation from Springfield, Massachusetts.

CHAPTER THREE

The Source

"It is a strange preoccupation, perhaps, that urge to know where a river begins."

—Robert Brittain

DURING THE GREAT DEPRESSION the Rockies swarmed with impoverished men prospecting for gold, even though they could not tell sandstone from granite. While stretching my legs in Denver one afternoon, I passed hardware stores offering gold-mining outfits for $4.50 a set, complete with gold pan, pick, shovel, and booklet of instructions. The crisp air, brilliant sky, and jagged ranges to the west told me that I was out West again.

It was a breezy July morning when I left Denver, with fresh showers blowing in from the Rockies. I shouldered my new packsack and hit the road again, headed for Grand Lake, high on the western slope of the Continental Divide. From all I could learn this lake was close to the ultimate source of the Colorado and would make a good starting point for my downhill river cruise.

SEVERAL RIDES BROUGHT ME to the old mining town of Empire by sunset. In stumbling through a pine grove in the dusk, intent on camping beside a roaring stream, I was startled to see two dim figures approaching me. They proved to be gold miners who had seen my flashlight through the trees. One of them, Jack Vaughn, invited me to spend the night in his cabin across the brook.

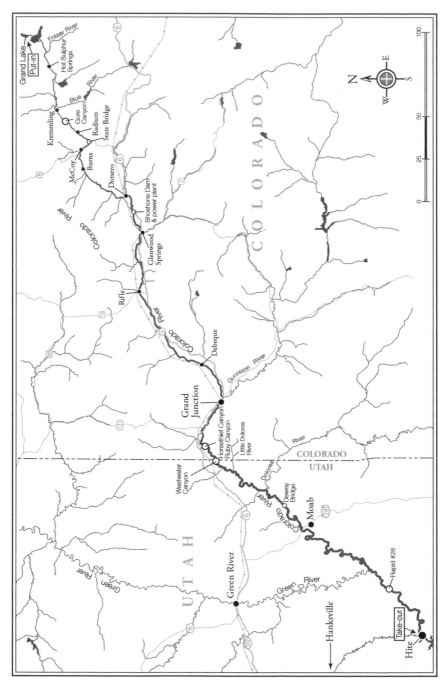

A map of Harold Leich's trip down the Colorado River, showing the put-in at Grand Lake and the take-out at Hite. Although technically Leich did not make it all the way to Hite in his handmade boat, he did walk and swim from the spot he wrecked his boat to Hite, where he departed the river to walk to Hanksville. It appears to many river historians today that he wrecked his boat between Rapid 28 and Rapid 24. Map by Thomas Child.

A 1933 view of the infant Colorado River near Lulu City in Grand County, Colorado.

Jack called me for a rugged breakfast the next morning—flapjacks, eggs, ham, and coffee. Our conversation continued long after the plates were empty. Jack was a professional miner who had piked into Alaska in the 1920s and came out with $35,000 from a mining venture, half of which he still had on reaching Seattle. The other half didn't last long, either. Now he was working alone in a tunnel seven hundred feet into the mountain, digging out gold and silver ore.

When Jack reluctantly went back into his mineshaft for a day's work, I climbed to the highway and walked towards the mountain crest amid abandoned tunnel openings. Soon a truck driver picked me up and took me to the top of Berthoud Pass, 11,300 feet above sea level. A trusting soul, he asked me to take over the wheel so he could nap beside me. We twisted down the road beneath snowy heights, passed the west portal of the Moffat tunnel, and came into the Fraser River valley, part of the Colorado watershed.

At the village of Granby, near the junction of the Fraser River with the upper Colorado, I learned that I had beaten my folding kayak out west. That afternoon I had my first glimpse of the infant Colorado. Those who have seen the vast torrent of mud in the Grand Canyon would scarcely recognize the clear little stream that dances through the meadows near Granby. Dazzled by the beauty of the green, sparkling river, I walked along its whitecapped waves for several miles.

In the evening a young salesman gave me a ride to Grand Lake. Just before sunset, when we approached the mountain walls near the lake, a heavy thunderstorm swept over us and dashed against the projecting ridges of the Rockies. A double rainbow leaped from the green valley to the summits and heralded my arrival from the swarming, sooty beehives of the east to the magnificence of the high country.

In Grand Lake village I found a room with Bill Walker, the local photographer, and then rowed around the lake in a tin rowboat. The lake was formed thousands of years ago when an alpine glacier pushed up a wall of rubble at the lower end of a narrow valley and then eventually melted away. High wooded slopes and bare cliffs rose from the eastern edge in a setting of great beauty, like a Norwegian fjord. But at the other end of the lake any wilderness feeling vanished in the fungoid excrescence of the village itself, a tin can tourist's paradise of hotdog stands and flimsy cottages filled with fat women in too-tight knickers, silk stockings, and high-heeled shoes—far different from the scene described by Major Powell in 1868, the summer before his first voyage through the Grand Canyon:

> A group of little alpine lakes, that receive their waters directly from per-petual snowbanks, discharge into a common reservoir, known as Grand Lake, a beautiful sheet of water. Its quiet surface reflects towering cliffs and crags of granite on its eastern shore; and stately pines and firs stand on its western margin.[1]

The next morning I started an argument among boatmen at the rental dock by asking about the true source of the Colorado. Most of them claimed that Grand Lake itself was the source, since its outlet stream flowed six miles southwest to pick up a stream called the North Fork. I knew they were mistaken, however, since Follansbee's report showed that the North Fork usually carried a larger volume of water; it headed up on the crest of the Never Summer Range some twenty miles north of the junction, where a few trickles of icy water mingled to form the true source of the Colorado.

Powell had considered Grand Lake the source of what was then called the Grand River (the Upper Colorado River of today), but he and others at that time called the Green River, originating in Wyoming, the source of the main Colorado.

With time on my hands until the boat arrived, I decided to see the river's source for myself and got a ride to the end of the North Fork road. There I met the summer ranger, Weenie Wilson, who offered to share his camp on the Continental Divide and to carry my gear up on his packhorse. I started ahead on foot and soon passed the long-abandoned mining camp of Lulu City, where roofless log cabins recalled a frenzied gold rush that began in 1879 and ended four years later when the ore ran out.

Next the trail climbed westward to an embankment high on the mountainside. At first this looked like a superhighway but it turned out to be a large diversion canal called the Grand River Ditch, which inter-cepted several brooks on the eastern slope of the Never Summer range and diverted them eight miles north into La Poudre Pass. There the flow entered a small lake exactly on the Continental Divide at an elevation of 10,200 feet, and cascaded down the Atlantic side of the watershed for the benefit of ranchers along the Cache la Poudre River. Each spring a gang of a dozen men worked for a month digging a channel through the packed snow to start the water flowing. Thus almost at its source the lifegiving water of the Colorado was snatched across the mountains into the Mississippi drainage.

The outer bank of the ditch formed a wide roadway following the contours of the escalloped mountainside. I longed for my kayak to float down the swift green current past soaring crags and fir-covered slopes. Late in the afternoon I reached camp on the lakelet in La Poudre Pass and soon Weenie and his assistant rode in behind me.

The lonely tent of Weenie's ranger post was the most remote in Rocky Mountain National Park; it was already mid-July and I was his first visitor. Weenie had manned the post for many summers. His regular job was coaching the University of Illinois football squad. I pitied the rookies who came against his 180 pounds of fighting beef after his summers of riding and climbing. At that time he was the only man who had climbed every peak of the Never Summer Range.

The next morning before I shoved off Weenie showed me a unique feature of his little lake. Most of the water, true enough, flowed over a lip on the northern end into the headwaters of the Cache La Poudre River, but at the other end a trickle found its way through a leaky wooden dam and flowed into the north fork of the Colorado—thus, the lakelet shared its waters between the Atlantic and the Pacific. Weenie assured me that I was at last at the genuine source of the Colorado.

My objective that morning was the summit of Mt. Richthofen, the highest of the Never Summer Range, which towered over the North Fork Valley. The name of this noble peak at the source of the Colorado seems strange on an American map, at least to my generation who grew up reading about "The Red Knight of Germany," Baron Manfred von Richthofen, credited with more victories than any other aviator of the First World War until he was shot down. Obviously the mountain was not named for him, but the curious fact is that two other barons of the same family were in the American West during the last century and for some time there was doubt about which one the mountain was named for. Ferdinand von Richthofen, a noted explorer and geologist, served as a volunteer with the Whitney Survey in California from 1862 to 1868, where he helped map the Comstock Lode. He also performed notable geological work in China. Walter von Richthofen came to Denver some years later and at one time planned to build an ambitious spa in the Rockies. Henry Gannett, also a member of the Whitney Survey, stated in a book published in 1902 that the mountain was named for the geologist.[2] Final proof is shown by the name of Richthofen Mountain in the atlas of the Clarence King Survey, published in 1876, the year before Walter arrived in Denver.[3]

To approach the summit I climbed through Skeleton Gulch, a glacial cirque where snowbanks still lay at the base of the headwall. High on a rocky spur, where the vertical bedrock emerged from a jumble of boulders, I passed an old mineshaft with a rusty wheelbarrow at the entrance and a pick, shovel, and pan as if they had just been dropped by a disappointed prospector. From there I picked the wrong chimney and had to do some real rock climbing to reach the sloping meadows near the top. In climbing the final rock cone I realized that a year of riding Pullmans was no preparation for high-altitude climbing. From Weenie's cairn at the summit I could trace the Upper Colorado from its headwaters basin below me until it disappeared to the southwest into the gateway of Gore Canyon, sixty miles in the purple distance. I wondered how my little boat would fare within its narrow walls.

Another overnight hike out of Grand Lake village took me to the top of Longs Peak, 14,245 feet high, the loftiest summit in Rocky Mountain National Park, and then the folding kayak finally arrived from Indiana. One morning the stage driver hauled it up from Granby and I spent the afternoon puzzling over the pieces. Two carrying bags spilled forth an assortment of hardwood rods, varnished frames, brass bolts, and frayed, rubberized canvas.

Lulu City, the site of an old mining camp visited by Harold Leich on the north fork of the Colorado River in Rocky Mountain National Park.

A booklet of instructions gave voluminous directions on page after page of fine German print, but each page had been translated into three or four words of typed English at the top. My two years of college German had imparted such essentials of the language as *zwei bier*, but did not include such canoeing terms as *sperrholzbordleiste* and *zapfenverbindung*.

The pieces of the kayak, as they lay in a heap on the grass, looked like some weird test of mechanical ingenuity. After an hour of fitting parts together one moment and taking them apart the next, I couldn't tell whether the thing I had bought was a boat or a collapsible birdcage. But finally a slim-decked hull rested on the grass and even the double-bladed paddles had been decollapsed.

I spent the next two days making a spray cover for the cockpit, since the boat had a large open area forward where the second paddler usually sat. I had already seen enough of the upper river to know that waves would flood over the cockpit coaming without such protection. I waterproofed the cloth with two coats of white paint and sewed a rope around the edge so the cover could be lashed down tightly.

Between get-ready chores I cruised around Grand Lake several times to see how the boat handled. Although she was a two-man craft, seventeen feet long, I found I could maneuver her well and attain a fair rate of speed.

At last one evening I felt ready to start the voyage; my gear was complete and ten days out of doors had improved my physical condition. I packed my

Harold and his folding kayak, the *Rob Roy*, at the outlet of Grand Lake at the start of his voyage.

The *Rob Roy* on shore two miles below Grand Lake, near the headwaters of the Colorado River.

A scenic shot of the river taken below Columbine Creek in the Arapaho National Forest, Colorado.

outfit that night in the hope of beginning the first complete voyage from the waters near the source of the Colorado River to the Gulf of California.

There is one subject on which I claim to be the world's leading authority: the vanished canoeing beauties of the Upper Colorado from Grand Lake down to what is now Granby Dam. No one can ever follow me, since the riverbed now lies on the bottom of Shadow Mountain Lake and Lake Granby. The irrigation ditch I saw in La Poudre Pass was just a modest forerunner of the vast Colorado–Big Thompson irrigation project, which captures the flow of the Upper Colorado and feeds it from Grand Lake thirteen miles through the Alva B. Adams Tunnel under the Continental Divide to the Big Thompson River on the eastern slope.

I offer the following account as a memorial to the vanished rivers of America—to the rocks and rills that have drowned in stagnant pools behind large dams. There will be many more such drownings in our nation's future. The least the river runners of our generation can do is describe these doomed streams for posterity.

On Friday, July 21, 1933, I carried the kayak to the shore of Grand Lake, loaded her up, and pushed away at 8:30 a.m. For cargo the boat held the packsack, a duffel bag, and the waterproof rubber sack holding maps, two cameras, and matches. The weight of the outfit compensated for the absence of a second crew member forward. Filled with anticipation for the

Above Granby and the Arapaho Bridge the river drops eighty-five feet within a mile. Hal ran this rocky stretch in the photo without portage or lining his boat.

Hal's kayak below Sleepy Hollow, near Trout Rapids on the Colorado River, with unidentified people next to the kayak.

excitement ahead, I pushed her along with the double-bladed paddle and steered for the lake's outlet.

As she glided across the water I thought of a passage from the journal of John MacGregor, one of the first to discover the delights of single-handed river cruising:

> Then the mind, placid in solitude, turned itself inwards, thinking of the length of the journey—the unknown difficulties to be met, the mysterious future of incidents to happen, the possible perils . . . the falls and deeps, the rapids and shallows, the waves and whirlpools, the upsets and groundings, the calms and breezes. These and all the other countless features of a lonely water journey . . . were all imagined with an eager, intense longing to meet them every one.

MacGregor, a retired Scottish minister, spent the latter years of his life cruising the waterways of Europe and the Near East in a decked canoe called the *Rob Roy*. In the 1860s and 1870s his keel plowed the Baltic, the Rhine, the Seine, and the Jordan. His little boat attracted crowds who could not understand how it survived surging rapids and ocean storms, and the voyager took advantage of their curiosity by handing them religious tracts. My rubber foldboat was a descendant of the *Rob Roy*, since its prototype was developed for the mountain streams of Bavaria from the kayak model that MacGregor used. It would be his turn to be astonished if he could see the rivers of Europe today with their thousands of foldboats, kayaks, and canoes plunging through swift water where his *Rob Roy* rode alone more than a century ago. I had fallen into the habit of thinking of my boat as another *Rob Roy* and finally decided to let that be her name.[4]

The weather was clear as the *Rob Roy* forged across the lake, and the dark green waters, 264 feet deep, sparkled in the sunshine. In a few moments, the boat glided under a footbridge across the lake's outlet stream and the swift current carried her into a shady tunnel. Although the deep, green water ran without a ripple, its speed was gratifying. A paddle stroke now and then to keep her bow out of a backwater was all that I needed to do. She gradually outdistanced a dude cowboy who was trotting along the bank.

On the evening before, I had talked to Captain McCarthy, the oldest boatman on the lake, about navigating the outlet stream. I bought a kapok cushion from him while he ate his supper in a cabin built over the lake. When I asked him if many boats had gone down the outlet he nearly choked on a morsel of food. "You'll find boats down there, my boy," was his cryptic reply.

I did find some "boats down there," several miles below the lake. They were weather-beaten hulks of ancient motorboats piled up along the banks,

The confluence of the Fraser River and the Colorado River below Granby, Colorado, looking toward Windy Gap.

but they seemed more like relics of the boneyard than marine casualties. Actually, the worst hazards to navigation that I found were barbed wire fences stretched across the water. Soon I pushed under the last one and joined the North Fork in a quiet meadow.

Where the two streams merged, the Grand Lake outlet was carrying a greater volume of water, although the North Fork must have been larger before its headwaters were diverted. Satisfied that I was somewhere near the head of navigation on the mighty Colorado, I pointed her bow downstream and prepared for the swift water that I could see ahead.

Below the confluence the combined currents whirled the boat past boulders and rock fragments that jutted through the rippling wavelets. The river left the meadowland with its pine-fringed shores and swung into a densely wooded gorge. Low mudbanks gave way to fir-clad ribs of rock and undercut cliffs. Often, I could not avoid submerged boulders, but with the force of the current behind her the kayak bumped along until she reached deeper water. Since I was sitting on the bottom I could feel each boulder pass under her flexible rubber skin.

Deeper in the gorge the rapids lengthened until there was scarcely any smooth water; the boat nosed between gravel bars, banks of large stones, and isolated boulders. Since the boat and the rapids were both new to me, my experience on the Yellowstone didn't help much. Here were no rock-free chutes but rather nests and traps of boulders. I tried at first to backpaddle and steer by swinging her stern in the direction I wanted to go. But the boulders strewn across the riverbed and the *Rob Roy*'s length of seventeen feet made this difficult. After an hour or so of ramming head-on into rocks that were high and dry, bumping over submerged boulders that I saw and feverishly tried to avoid, and standing athwart the channel, I decided to change my tactics.

Gradually I began a head-on, offensive attack. When I entered a rapid with some forward speed, I found I could steer with the paddle, veer from side to side as the channel required, and have enough steerage way to make a sharp turn. When the little river rounded a bend and the curving rapids crowded against the bank, I could lean on the paddle and swing around the inside of the bend like pivoting on a ski pole.

I landed for lunch below Columbine Creek, near a cliff that rose in a sheer wall from the river. On resuming my ride I soon lost any confidence remaining from the morning's run. The boat found herself in a wild, roaring stretch of whitewater, with large boulders rising six or eight feet above the torrent. How she got through was more than I could account for. I could take no credit for it, since the river treated the boat more kindly than my handling of her deserved.

The kayak proved herself a rough-water bronco, riding over foaming waves and weaving through tortuous passages that must have looked impossible from shore. Losing altitude rapidly, I tried to steer as best I could through twisting channels. She took some hard knocks along her keel and scraped her gunwales frequently on rocks and boulders, but stood up well because of her elastic hide and springy framework. Her slick wet rubber bottom slid nicely over polished stones.

In the mile just above Arapaho Creek the river fell about eighty-five feet, a terrific drop on any stream. The most dangerous canyons of the middle Colorado have a fall of about thirty-five feet to the mile, but there the much greater volume of water enormously increases the hazard. I had intended to walk alongshore in this section and let the boat down by a line, but I got so busy trying to pick a clear channel that I did not realize how close the Arapaho was. Suddenly I glanced ahead and saw the bridge across the Colorado near the mouth of the creek. The river below me spurted into a churning mass of whitewater, wherever I could see it among a field of boulders. The current did not allow me to land. It sucked the boat around large rocks, through roaring chutes, and over hidden ledges in a wild runaway ride, bumping, scraping, and pitching.

Beneath the bridge came the best fun—a narrow flume into which most of the current funneled. Just below the bridge this flume spewed its flow against a large boulder and the current made a sharp turn to the right. The boat danced swiftly through the flume, careened around the curve, and ran her nose into a quiet pool below.

From Arapaho Creek I paddled down the Colorado's augmented flow through a delightful open valley called Sleepy Hollow. In a few hundred yards the character of the river changed completely; instead of steep, rock-filled rapids I found a clear channel winding from bank to bank, sparkling with green and whitecapped waves. I enjoyed bouncing down the rock-free riffles and watching the sagebrush-covered hills of Sleepy Hollow slip past the gunwales. This was kayaking at its best; the boat slapped through the curling crests with exhilarating speed and grace. Pebbles and small boulders on the riverbed showed clearly through the shallow green water. Swift runs curving between low shores carried the *Rob Roy* around one bend after another, sometimes giving a view back to the hills along the Arapaho and sometimes confronting the rocky gate of a small gorge at the lower end of Sleepy Hollow. This cleft was already designated as a future dam site, listed in Follansbee's book as "Hine No. 2 (Lehman) Site," and here is where Granby Dam now blocks the channel.

Soon the boat drifted with the current into the gorge, the first and smallest canyon of the Colorado, the forerunner of chasms that become deeper, longer, and steeper until they lead into the depths of the Grand Canyon. The waves dashed over the deck, flooded over my new spray cover, and found a way inside the kayak. On a patch of shore halfway through the gorge I stopped at a little ranch house to catch my breath and bail out some water. Two children were so intrigued by this performance that I was careful not to disappoint my first gallery during the next stretch.

Soon the valley widened into green meadowland where the rushing river curved in graceful swoops across the flats. Around one bend I found a fallen tree blocking the main channel; most of the flow swirled into a net of tangled branches. By a frantic effort I leaned on the paddle and rode the inside of the riffle safely around the bend.

As it approached the mouth of the Fraser River, the Colorado sprawled among gravel bars and almost lost itself in a maze of small, braided channels. Luckily I made a good choice and sailed through without having to get out and push, although there would not have been room for another boat alongside mine.

Doubled by the Fraser's flow, the river ran through swift riffles into Windy Gap, a shallow cut in a range of hills and the next gorge in the Colorado series. Behind me I had a last view of the Continental Divide and its jagged peaks, and realized that I was well started on the eight-thousand-foot drop to sea level. A brief thunder squall blew upstream and then the sun broke under the clouds to color the rocky hills a deep orange.

Early in the evening I began passing ranch houses along the shores and soon I reached the village of Hot Sulphur Springs, at the head of Byers Canyon. Pulling alongshore above the highway bridge, I landed among a crowd of spectators whose curiosity indicated how few boats had traveled this section of the river. I knew how John MacGregor must have felt on his voyages, when the original *Rob Roy* was the center of great crowds wherever he landed. The editor of the local newspaper, Wallace Houston, volunteered to help me carry the boat up a steep bank to the street. After we had stored her in an empty shop for the night I found a room in a hotel on the riverbank.

I felt satisfied with the first day's voyage despite the frequent encounters with boulders. I had dropped 709 feet in elevation in 31 miles without taking the boat out of the water, from Grand Lake at 8,369 feet to Hot Sulphur Springs at 7,660 feet, an average drop of 22 feet per mile. It would not take long to reach sea level at that rate. *Rob Roy* had begun the day on a stream no larger than a trout brook and had followed it until it was a roaring river. In fact, the subdued grumble coming from the depths of Byers Canyon warned me of the river's power.

CHAPTER FOUR

In the Wake of Sam Adams

IN BYERS CANYON the Colorado has cut its way into a low range of hills west of Hot Sulphur Springs until the river is a slender green and white ribbon in the bottom of a narrow trough. The canyon is named for William N. Byers, pioneer editor of the *Rocky Mountain News*, who owned tracts of land in the area. In 1868 he and Major Powell led the first party to the summit of Longs Peak.

On Saturday morning I looked over the canyon rapids from a new highway halfway up the southern wall. Two men from the village drove me along the road while they told vivid tales of the river's dangers. No one had ever taken a boat through the canyon, they said, and the only person who tried gave up after nearly losing his boat. This adventurer, variously described as a German, Russian, or Swede, had appeared with a folding kayak like mine several years before and was last seen boarding the train after his losing bout with the rapids. I was to hear more of this mysterious stranger lower on the river.

From what I saw of the canyon I felt that *Rob Roy* could make it, although the run would be by far the worst I had ever tried. In three places the cataracts were steep enough to be called falls. Sections of the river dropped in continuous rapids for a quarter of a mile, studded with angular rocks and boiling through narrow flumes.

Back at Hot Sulphur Springs several townsmen helped me carry my outfit down to the river. I left a camera with them so they could take photos of the boat in the rapids. Then I loaded up, strapped the kapok cushion onto my shoulders, lashed down the spray cover, and pushed off into the swift green current. Word had spread that another nut was going to try the canyon, for most of the village was on hand to see me start. Amid questions about where I wanted my body shipped, I sailed under the bridge and turned sharply to the right into the canyon. Most of the spectators followed me in cars along the highway, although some had already picked vantage points above the steepest cataracts to watch the sport. It looked like a Roman holiday for Hot Sulphur Springs.

In the gloomy gateway the narrow river increased its speed, rushing along in glassy, dark green ripples. Ordinarily I would have enjoyed the swift ride, but a feeling of nervousness robbed me of any pleasure (the fact is, I was scared). Soon the surface broke into foam as the river dropped over the rough canyon bottom. *Rob Roy* rode the waves easily, her bow bobbing through the swells and her spray cover shedding buckets of water.

IN A MOMENT I COULD SEE where the first falls dropped ahead. A sharp rock jutted from the water near the right bank and on its downstream side the river disappeared. Instead of landing to inspect the place as caution dictated, I played to the gallery and headed for the narrow chute between the rock and the right bank. I then abandoned my offensive attack and backed water in the current, thinking I could look over the chute before going through. But as the *Rob Roy* lost steerage way I suddenly realized my error and tried to straighten her out so she could enter the chute head

Hal navigated hard, fast water in Byers Canyon, Grand County, Colorado.

Hal recorded this as the worst stretch of rapids in Byers Canyon, where he lined about eighty yards and ran the rest.

The *Rob Roy* in Byers Canyon.

Hal stopped to dry his gear below Byers Canyon.

on. It was already too late—she drifted broadside against the rock, tilted downstream, and spilled me into the pool below in a neat nose dive over the jagged pinnacle.

I rose quickly to the surface of the cold pool, thanks to the life preserver cushion on my back. I saw *Rob Roy* floating past me upside down. Grabbing the paddle as it drifted by, I straddled the stern of the kayak and brought her ashore below the outrun of the cataract. High on the road on the opposite wall dozens of people shouted and waved their arms. My mood did not improve when I looked back at the falls and saw that the left-hand channel would have given me a clear but rough passage. My carelessness had brought its proper penalty.

The only satisfaction I got out of the incident was in righting the boat and bailing her out without help; in half an hour she was ready for some more rapids. My self-confidence, however, was badly shaken, and the worst water still lay ahead. Resolving to make no more plays to the grandstand, I stripped off my soggy clothing down to my shorts and climbed aboard.

A hundred yards below, I landed on the left bank at the head of the worst water in the canyon, a broken jumble of rock and foam that stretched down the river about a quarter of a mile. After a long look I decided to let the boat down by a line for the first fifty yards. This worked well enough for a short distance, until I came to a wall of rock rising vertically from the

The confluence of the Blue and Colorado Rivers at Kremmling, Colorado, shows a slow river backed up by the narrow entrance to Gore Canyon, six miles downstream.

foam. There the only possible passage was to reembark and try to keep out of the main channel, a wild mass of whitewater.

With the stern rope in my teeth, I paddled carefully under the cliff and jumped ashore on the first point of rocks. With feet planted on the bank it was all I could do to hold the stern line as the boat sucked and tugged in the strong current. For the next ten yards I picked my way down the shore, fearing at every moment that the boat would be swept from my control. Then I reached a stretch that seemed possible to run. I jumped aboard and sailed through the whitewater better than I had expected, amid the tooting of horns and the roar of the crowd.

A few yards of calm water gave me a breather before the last bad section. Caution called for lining the boat around a waterfall at the upper end. Then I nosed out into midstream and let the boat go whooping down the turbulent rapids. The whitewater ended in a final plunge over two boulders, a fall of about four feet, much like the spot where I had capsized. Again I hit the rock on the right-hand side and swung athwart the current. *Rob Roy* leaned over dangerously, but just as I was preparing myself for another cold plunge, she scraped her way around the rock into the middle channel and was sucked over the waterfall right side up, buried in foam.

The rest of the canyon was easy, a deep sluiceway with many large waves but no rocks. My anxiety gone, I settled back to enjoy a roller coaster ride through the breakers. The *Rob Roy* must have been a sight from shore as she leaped out of wave crests half her length and sank into the troughs until she nearly disappeared. Shaking the green water off her decks, she would rise to the next swell and curtsy and dip in a slow rhythm. I was disappointed to see smooth water ahead in approaching the highway bridge that marked the lower end of the canyon. I landed below the bridge at 11:50 a.m., having started into the canyon at 10:30.

My friends wished me luck, returning the camera and packsack they had carried for me. While my clothing dried in the hot sunlight, I ate lunch and looked at maps of the river ahead. To make up for the rugged morning, the afternoon was a dream. I found swift, splashy little riffles, thunderstorms to make things interesting, and a constant variety of scenery. This was Middle Park, so named by "the Pathfinder," John C. Fremont, on his 1843 expedition because it was a fairly level vale amid the mountain flanks. Similar areas nearby are called North Park, South Park, and Estes Park. By a fluke of geography, Middle Park was not official American territory when I ran its riffles. Historians discovered that these bountiful few thousand acres had never been formally acquired by our government; the Louisiana Purchase extended to its eastern side and the territory ceded by Spain began at its western edge! At last the governor of Colorado brought it into the United States during a flag-raising ceremony at Breckenridge, Colorado, on August 9, 1936.

Looking downriver at the portal to Gore Canyon, below Kremmling, Colorado.

Whether a "no man's land" or not, I loved Middle Park with its broad vistas towards snowcapped ranges, its arid sagebrush hills, and the swift green river winding through it. When the afternoon storms cleared I could see a massive bulk rising ahead, the Gore Range (or the Park Range on some maps), which blocked off Middle Park at its western edge. That meant the beginning of some grim canyon country.

Just before sunset I camped on a grassy bank opposite the mouth of the Blue River, some twenty-seven miles below Hot Sulphur Springs. Here both rivers lie in glassy pools between low shores of meadowland, scarcely hinting at the frenzied rapids their waters have already churned through or at the far worse cataracts that extend below. This undramatic confluence nonetheless witnessed a little drama of the American West a century ago. Captain Samuel Adams, a small-time politician from Arizona, came down the Blue River to this point in 1869 in a small flotilla seeking an easy water route to California. His stock-in-trade was the legend of a potentially fruitful paradise in the arid lands of the Southwest, and he aimed to show the nation that the Colorado valley could become a river highway and a rail route for opening up this new territory.

Adams had actually taken an easy raft trip of eleven miles on the lower Colorado, below the Grand Canyon, and had attempted to get federal support for further explorations. He tried to join Major Powell's Colorado River expedition when it was starting into the canyons from Green River, Wyoming, in May 1869, but the major was not impressed by his credentials and sent him on his way. Adams then went to Breckenridge, near the head of the Blue River, where he persuaded some miners to join him in an expedition down the water-level route to the Pacific. He must have been a master salesman, for the little mining camp gave him financial support and a glorious farewell.

Reality came quickly in the rapids of the Blue River, with repeated capsizing and loss of equipment. Twelve days after the parting speeches at Breckenridge, three of the original four open boats sailed down to the calm waters at the Colorado confluence, across from the bank where I was now camping, and five of the original party had finished the trip back to Breckenridge on foot. But Sam Adams's hopes must have soared when he entered the placid little Colorado, like a barge canal for some miles above and below the Blue River junction. His only remaining problem was that the river elevation at the junction was 7,335 feet above the

Hal decided to portage about fifty feet around this bad fall in Gore Canyon.

Pacific Ocean, and barge canals don't drop down that fast—not without expensive locks.

After supper by the Blue River, a mile's walk across the flats brought me to the town of Kremmling, where I milled around with the Saturday night crowd of ranchers, railroad section hands, and prospectors. I loafed on the riverbank Sunday morning while the contents of my duffel bag, soaked in Byers Canyon, dried in the sun.

On the river again, I followed in the wake of Sam Adams's flotilla in the general direction of California. It was a slow six-mile grind pushing the loaded kayak around calm meanders; in the nine miles above Gore Canyon the river does not drop a single foot. The resistant rock across the canyon's mouth acts like a dam backing up a long lake.

Early in the afternoon I landed at the head of the canyon and walked along the railroad track on the north shore to look it over. I had no illusions about running the entire stretch, for the map had already told me that the river drops more than 100 feet to the mile for a short section, with a total fall of 360 feet in five miles. Follansbee's report described four major dam sites in the first thousand feet below the canyon's entrance.

At Gore Canyon the river has cut a winding gash through contorted red rock, a gneiss laced by veins of quartz. Its walls are sparsely covered with cedars—in fact, Cedar Canyon was its original name. The railroad

A scenic photograph of Gore Canyon, composed by Hal during his river trip.

follows the gorge along high embankments, passing through several tunnels and deep cuts. The tracks enter the canyon a few feet above water level and descend steadily, but when they leave the lower end they cut high on the canyon side, so great is the river's descent. The walls rise nearly vertically for five hundred feet and slope up for another five hundred feet.

The canyon represents a classic example of downcutting by a powerful stream and in this respect is typical of other Colorado River canyons. By looking at a topographic map it is easy to see that the river was there first and that the Gore Range slowly rose beneath it. By its abrasive action in rolling boulders along its bed, the river acted like a giant rasp and cut a thousand feet into the hard, red rock, as fast as the mountains rose. It is likely that the water volume and therefore the cutting effect was greater at the end of the last ice age than it is today, but in any case the cutting must have taken millions of years. If the mountain had risen faster than the river could cut, the Colorado would have backed up and the drainage pattern would be far different today.

One of Major Powell's chief contributions to the emerging science of geology came from his observations of river erosion in the Colorado basin. He used the term "antecedent" stream to describe ancient rivers like the Colorado that continued their old courses when the land rose beneath them. He held that river canyons resulted from long ages of erosion; here he differed from the catastrophe school of scientists, who thought that mountains and canyons were caused by sudden upheavals of nature.

After my track-side reconnaissance of Gore Canyon, I returned convinced that *Rob Roy* could ride the first mile successfully, except for one ten-foot fall that would require a portage. With the spray cover tightly lashed, I paddled across the calm surface to the canyon entrance. There the whole river narrowed to five or six yards and sank in a V-shaped tongue into a mass of foaming waves. She dipped her nose into the trough and fought to rise over the breakers. Beyond the fourth big haystack the whole river bulged over a sunken ledge, forming a fall on the downstream side. She rode over the hump of water beautifully and then plunged into the foam and nearly foundered, burying herself for three-quarters of her length. Solid water as well as foam came aboard, for the spray cover sagged and water rushed into the cockpit. At the same time the brass clamps of the framing loosened, causing the ladder-like keel structure to buckle beneath me.

I now awoke to the fact that I was in a most uncomfortable position. The rapids stretched ahead for another hundred yards and my collapsible boat, half full of water, was collapsing around me. I managed to steer closer to shore, where I jumped onto a boulder and snubbed the stern line around a projecting rock. My old felt hat, still showing traces of soot from my days as a traveling man, served as an emergency bailing bucket. I lashed down the keel structure as best I could, cast off, and rode the remaining rapids safely, curving around in a wide, S-shaped bend.

Below the rapids I slowed down to avoid being drawn over the ten-foot fall. Luckily a narrow ledge on the left allowed a precarious portage. As I loaded up again by the wide plunge pool below the fall, a young prospector shouted and waved from the other bank. I crossed over to him and learned, above the roar of the waterfall, that he was warning me of the dangerous water ahead. Although fully prepared for the worst descent, I thanked him for his kindness. He watched me run the riffles to the head of the bad water.

Here the Colorado went mad. Niagara Gorge below the falls, with its rock-free channel, would be easy by comparison. The river drops for over two miles in a continuous cataract through a narrow, boulder-strewn gorge, like a little mountain cascade leaping over pebbles but magnified a thousand times. And here it was that Sam Adams's California expedition shattered on the foam-lashed boulders of what he called the "Grand Cannon." One after another, his three remaining boats were lost—not in attempting to run the cataracts, for even these argonauts were not that foolhardy—but merely in the effort to line them downstream from the steep and rocky shore. Food supplies and equipment also went down the roaring gulch.

By this time most of the miners were walking home, and only the resolute captain and five of his crew remained to build a raft of driftwood and continue the voyage. But in a short distance the raft disintegrated too and three more of the miners headed for home.

Now the expedition had dwindled to the misguided but indomitable Adams, two loyal followers, and some waterlogged provisions. In succession they built and lost three more rafts, until even these courageous water rats gave up and started walking back upstream. Adams claimed they had reached a point about sixty miles downstream from Cedar (now Gore) Canyon when the fourth raft dissolved into driftwood, but in view of his uniformly exaggerated estimates it is not possible to tell how far he actually got—maybe to Red Gorge or Rouge Canyon.

Sometime during these last days of his rafting cruise, Captain Adams climbed a rocky hillside, gazed towards California, and recorded the view in his journal:

> Three years before as I stated in my Report to the Sec of War, I looked up the Colorado River from a point 650 miles from its mouth and could see a vally exten [sic] 75 miles to the NE. I could now look to the SW & almost see the narrow gap which divided us.[1]

He was claiming, in other words, to have seen all the way across western Colorado, part of Utah, and most of Arizona, from an outlying ridge of the Rockies to a point west of the Grand Canyon—some five hundred miles in an airline. Despite his catastrophic voyage, he was still convinced that he had discovered an easy passage to the West, "The Great Natural Thoroughfare of Arizona and Utah." For years he pressed his claims for reimbursement and for recognition, with letters to successive secretaries of war, with a concurrent resolution of the Nevada Territory to support him, and with petitions to Congress. But for all his courage, effort, and misguided energy, in 1875 the Senate Committee on Claims wrecked his hopes for good in the concluding acerbic words of its Report No. 662:

> The whole paper is a complex tissue [sic] of errors and exaggerations. He starts on his voyage down the Blue, 700 feet above the highest peak of the Rocky Mountains. He discovers fields of wild grain, unknown to the botanists of North America. He discovers mines of precious metals of fabulous wealth. He states that those opposed to his exploration of the Colorado River cut down the timber along its banks, so that he could procure no fuel for his boat, etc.
>
> Mr. Adams has made no map of any part of the Colorado River, or any of its tributaries. He has determined no latitude or longitude, and no altitude, and in describing parts which he has probably seen he often errs in giving correct position by several hundred miles. Whatever may have been the services of Mr. Adams, they were rendered without any authority of law, and your committee seeing no reason why the Government should be called upon to pay for them, report back the bill referred to them, and recommend that it be indefinitely postponed.[2]

During that same summer of 1869, the Powell expedition was threading the tortuous canyons of the Green River and the main Colorado, culminating in the first voyage through the Grand Canyon. Powell's visits to Middle Park in 1867 and 1868 no doubt convinced him of the impossibility of taking boats through what he knew as Cedar Canyon, and in any case the new railroad access at Green River, Wyoming, made his outfitting task that much simpler.

At the head of Gore Canyon I was finally going beyond Powell's footsteps. I had followed them from Denver to Empire, over Berthoud Pass to Grand Lake, up Longs Peak, into Middle Park, and to the place where I currently stood on the shore. But from there he had turned north in 1868 and cut across the plateau to the Green River country.

So the high cliffs of Gore Canyon saw Powell, the one-armed Civil War major, en route to his destiny as explorer and scientist, and the fantastic Adams en route to nowhere. The name of the canyon and the range through which it cuts recalls another fabulous character who passed this way in the nineteenth century: Sir George Gore, an Irish baronet. In 1855 he mounted an enormous hunting expedition to the Rockies, with a retinue of 40 retainers, 14 dogs, 112 horses, and 6 wagons. He was so disappointed when his men struck gold that he moved camp at once, shouting, "I did not come here to seek gold! I don't need it. This is a pleasure hunt."

When the American Fur Company asked too much freight to ship out his hides, he burned the hides and his wagons too. The "pleasure hunt" bagged three thousand buffalo and forty grizzly bears in North, South, and Middle Parks. So wanton was the slaughter that a Native American tribe nearly attacked the hunters in protest. The red rocks of Gore Canyon coupled with the accidental appropriateness of its name memorialize this bloody moment of Sir George's pleasure.

Coming back from the nineteenth century to July 1933, I had my troubles too. The young prospector, Werner Greger of Parshall, helped me carry the boat along the railroad grade for a mile and a quarter, just beyond Tunnel 37. There I thought I could line her through the remaining rough section, so we lifted her gently down a steep rocky slope to the river. The last hour before dark found me lining the empty boat downstream. The bobbing kayak was almost unmanageable in the heavy waves—like the Scottish outlaw for whom the boat was named, *Rob Roy* wanted to cut loose and have full independence.

After dark the roaring river, beating itself into a lather on ledges and boulders, gleamed with an eerie light in the bottom of the gorge. In Kremmling they still talked of the days when the railroad was being hewn through the canyon and how workers sometimes fell into the torrent during high water, or were pushed in at night after an evening brawl in town.

In climbing up the slope to my camping gear, I stumbled in the dark against an old barrel and ran a rusty nail an inch into my hand. I camped in a ditch beside the track on the only level spot I could find. After the exertions of the day, I had no trouble sleeping despite the cinders under my blanket. I woke up once when a freight train rumbled by and blew steam in my face. The next morning my hand was beginning to swell. I started walking back the six miles to Kremmling and for the last mile got a ride on a little gasoline car with the section boss. The town's only doctor opened up the wound and inserted a drain. He gave me some extras and assured me I would have no trouble if I changed the dressing occasionally.

It was 1:00 by the time I walked back to my camp. I spent the rest of the day maneuvering *Rob Roy* along the rocky shore to the foot of the canyon. I would let her shoot out in the current for a yard or two and then brace myself to snub her with the line. Bucking and rearing like a bull on a tether, she seemed eager to take her chances in the cataracts. Once I let her drift down the full length of the line around a boulder as big as a house, expecting that I could bring her ashore on the downstream side. I tied the end to a rock, scrambled around the boulder, and was horrified to find that the boat had disappeared. Back on the upstream side again I saw that the rope sank under the rock. For a moment it looked like the end of the trip, but a hard tug on the line brought her out from her hiding place—an undercut cove on the river side of the boulder. The only solution was to carry her uphill a few yards and then down across a field of sharp rocks to the river. She took a worse pounding than in the rapids, for I often lost my footing and dropped her onto jagged rocks.

At rare intervals I could ride in the boat for a few yards at a time, through the less turbulent stretches. I would crouch with the stern line in my teeth, paddle close inshore to the next downward plunge, and then jump for the rocks and snub her as she dropped over the falls. Finally, I reached the end of the cataracts after making only a mile all afternoon. I walked back for my gear and at 6:30 pushed off from the mouth of Canyon Creek. Soon I emerged into the evening sunlight, out of the slot at the foot of Gore Canyon. Three hard rapids in the next mile warned me that something was seriously wrong with the *Rob Roy*—she steered like a waterlogged coal barge.

Spotting a fine campsite on a gravel bar across from a row of cliffs, I tied up for the night on the right bank, after a day's run of only 2¾ miles. My diary for July 24 shows plainly enough how I was beginning to feel about the kayak:

> Glad to leave Gore Canyon behind and wondering how Rob Roy will stand the water ahead. Would like to get her as far as Glenwood Springs, but she is cracking up fast. Three longitudinal braces are snapped off and the skin is wearing down to the canvas. It is easy to see that she is not built for this heavy water. Her 17-foot length makes her tough to steer, and I must admit that there are times when I lose control altogether.

CHAPTER FIVE

Idylls of a River Rat

I AWOKE THE NEXT MORNING under a brilliantly clear blue sky and rolled over in my blanket to see the green river sparkling beneath rugged cliffs. In reaching for my clothes, which I had thrown aside in a soggy heap the night before, I found they had dried out completely in the arid climate.

After breakfast I walked to the railroad section house in the town of Azure to borrow some twine. Then I pulled *Rob Roy* out on a gravel bar for a complete overhauling. The forward section proved to be a sorry mess indeed; the entire bow assembly had come apart, letting the rubber hull sag and bulge. No wonder she had been hard to steer in the last rapids of Gore Canyon. The forward transverse frame was shattered, one longitudinal brace was broken in three places, and two other braces were badly cracked.

I got to work about 11:00 and stayed on the job until after 2:00. Using splints of green wood, I crudely spliced the broken rods with twine. In reassembling the framework I lashed all connections with rawhide and tied down the keel assembly to keep it from buckling again. The good Bavarian craftsmen who had built the kayak many years before would have been shocked to see their handiwork. The repair job was like mending a precision scale with baling wire or polishing a camera lens with sandpaper.

Still, the boat was now rigid enough to steer easily. I paddled away from the cliffs of Azure camp at 3:30, wondering what sort of water lay ahead in Blacktail Canyon. The profile map showed an average fall of twenty to thirty feet per mile all the way down to the Glenwood Canyon dam. The

Here, the *Rob Roy* is shown in dry dock at Hal's Azure camp. He was making repairs after
the boat was damaged by the rapids and rocks of Gore Canyon.

descent in Blacktail Canyon was a little more; thus, I figured if I could pass through safely I need not worry about getting to Glenwood Springs.

In a few miles I landed at the entrance of Blacktail Canyon and found it a beautiful winding gorge with low but steep rocky sides. After looking over the first rapids I pushed off and sailed through the surges buoyantly. It was an idyllic run down a tumbling river that flowed between clean rock walls. I counted about five strong rapids, all of them nearly free of rocks. But there were enough hazards to make the run enjoyable; swift water boiling between perpendicular walls, white-crested waves surging against the current and then breaking into foam, and one beautiful bend to the left under a high cliff, where the tossing swells pushed close to the jagged shore. *Rob Roy* rode through superbly; it heartened me to know that her weakened framework could survive a drop of thirty feet to the mile with a good volume of water.

Below the canyon the boat rounded a rocky cape and sailed by two placer miners who were scrabbling onto the bank. One grizzled old fellow recovered himself enough to ask where I had come from. When I shouted back "Grand Lake" he stared in astonishment.

The valley widened into an open glen, in the center of which gleamed a white little village called Radium. I tied up at the bridge, five miles below Azure, and walked into town for supplies. Although there was no store, I bought a loaf of bread from the postmistress and some canned goods at the railroad section house. They had been watching the river for drifting wreckage ever since the train crews had reported a boat in Gore Canyon. When I asked about Red Gorge, the next canyon of the Colorado series, the postmistress pointed out an old man fishing from a rock, saying he had once run the ferry and would be glad to warn anyone foolish enough to try Red Gorge.

When I got to the old ferryman I swung into a whirlpool and asked him about the water below. He told me that Red Gorge was only slightly less dangerous than Gore Canyon and that it was full of cascades and boulders. In his fifty years in the region he had never heard of a successful voyage through Blacktail Canyon or Red Gorge.

I reached the entrance in another mile and found it a deep cut through brilliant red rock, quite similar to Gore Canyon. Fortunately the river's descent is milder. After surveying the first rapids from shore I paddled into the shadow of a high wall and plunged through the canyon without landing again. It proved to be a magnificent run: fast, thrilling, and just rough enough to be exciting in a low-lying kayak.

Halfway through, where the river divided around a rocky island, I ran a fast chute under an overhanging cliff on the left bank, sinking down a steep slope of water with exhilarating speed. Below the drop I passed an abandoned diversion tunnel, with twisted pipes and rusty beams half-submerged along the shore. This wreckage was all that remained from an attempt to build a dam in Red Gorge some thirty years before. The railroad had defeated the project, which would have submerged its track. Thus, one of the best swift-water runs on the upper river was saved.

Slapping along through high curling waves, *Rob Roy* dropped down to the foot of Red Gorge and sailed out into an open valley in the orange glow of the setting sun. The country was wilder than the settled glen at Radium; deserted slopes rose to rugged cliffs of red and yellow rock and with every mile the country seemed more arid, with more dusty green sagebrush and fewer dark green pines and cedars. In this region the lack of rainfall at lower elevations explains the absence of forest growth below 7,500 feet.

The cumulative effect of the Colorado's scenic power overwhelmed me. The canyons and vales had followed one another in a rhythmic pattern: the rocky cleft below the Arapaho and the open meadowland following it; Windy Gap and the pleasant valley above Hot Sulphur Springs; Byers Canyon and the western meadows of Middle Park; Gore Canyon and the delightful vale at Azure; Blacktail Canyon and the open Radium valley; and finally Red Gorge and the superb countryside through which I was now cruising.

I pitched camp on a sandy bank across from an undercut red sandstone cliff, only eight and a half miles from Azure. For supper I stewed some canned tuna, peas, and bacon—something of a chowder—and then sat by the fire and played a harmonica while the cliff echoed my tunes. A great blue heron felt the instrument was misnamed, for it circled the opposite shore venting raucous squawks of disgust.

A leisurely breakfast and a lazy morning around camp delayed my departure until 10:30. It was another idyllic journey, with swift water all the way. In an hour I reached the town of Yarmony, where three gandy dancers worked along the railroad track.

"How far to McCoy?" I yelled as *Rob Roy* swept below them.

"What?" they sang in a perfect chord like a Gilbert and Sullivan chorus.

"How far to McCoy?"

"Nine miles, but you'll never get there in that little thing."

"Why not?"

"Too much riffles down there!"

The "too much riffles" proved delightful sailing. *Rob Roy* didn't take a drop of water inside, although the spray cover was frequently soaked. In riding the stream, I wondered why so few others had discovered the delights of the Upper Colorado River. The local people looked on the river with dread, considering it a monster ready to devour everything within reach rather than a medium for an exhilarating sport. Whitewater running is a pleasure that is hard to analyze, and in any case does not appeal to the practical and the cautious. Its fascination may come from a feeling of mastery over a powerful force of nature, a physical delight in the violent motion, and a certain sense of fear. Like skiing, gravity supplies the motive force, and all you need do for your enjoyment is control the speed liberally provided by nature. In a kayak, the feeling of speed is accentuated because you are seated below the water level and almost seem to be a part of the current.

One fast, curving run that *Rob Roy* descended through high-crested waves must have looked exciting from shore. When I was halfway down, shooting a flume around a boulder, I heard a tremendous shouting above the sound of crashing water. A glance over my shoulder showed a group of placer miners on the left bank. They invited me for a visit, so I crossed the stream by stretching at full length in a narrow iron trough that was hauled across the current as part of their conveyor system.

"I'm Howard Tweed," the boss of the outfit told me after I had explained my fluvial mission. "And these fellows are my partners in a deal to wash down the riverbank for placer gold. This gravel pays off at a dollar a ton and there may be some richer stuff around too. You'd starve to death panning it by hand, but we're hooked up to a little brook and can sluice a lot of dirt through here in one day, working as a team."

One of the group showed me how to pan gold by hand. He squatted by the river and let some water swirl in his pan with a few handfuls of dirt. As he separated the coarser bits he threw them away and finally had a small amount of black sand left. Gleaming among the dark grains were four "colors," or flakes of free gold—the tiny fascinating sparks that led to the settlement of the American West.

At noontime the crew invited me into the cookshack for a hearty meal. One of them wanted to go with me on a cruise down the canyons of the Yampa River, in northwestern Colorado, where he said there were untouched sandbars of placer gold. Still curious about my predecessors, I asked whether they knew of any previous voyages down this section. Tweed replied, "The only fellow I ever saw adrift in those rapids was a miner who was sucked into the waves when he tried to paddle across in a sluice box. It's lucky we were here to fish him out."

The cordiality of Tweed and his crew typified the welcome that I found everywhere along the Colorado. After promising to send them copies of my pictures, I soared over the rapids in the aerial tramway and continued my journey.

After lunch I sailed past the town of State Bridge and soon reached Orestod, where the Denver and Salt Lake Railroad left the river. While backing water in an eddy I talked to a hobo who was stewing a can of mulligan beneath the water tank. He wanted a free ride forty miles downstream to Dotsero, where he hoped to have better luck riding the Denver and Rio Grande line. When I told him about the rapids ahead, he agreed that it would be better to ride the rails.

In another mile *Rob Roy* came to a brush-burning operation on the left bank, the first evidence of the Dotsero cutoff project to join the Denver and Salt Lake line with the Denver and Rio Grande Western. I had been

A stretch of the Colorado River in Rouge Canyon, Eagle County, Colorado.

Hal often used his kayak for scale and composition in his photographs, such as this one in Rouge Canyon on the Colorado River.

A view of the Colorado River below Red Dirt Creek in Eagle County, Colorado.

reading about this in the financial pages of the New York papers during my last days as a traveling man. The project was perhaps the last piece of transcontinental rail construction that our country would ever see. By building forty miles of track down the Colorado from Orestod to Dotsero, the two roads merged their lines, placed Denver on the main line of a transcontinental route, reduced the mileage between Denver and Salt Lake City by 170 miles, gave the Salt Lake rail line long-deferred access to the city for which it was named, and vindicated the $18 million Moffat Tunnel, which on its completion in 1923 merely led to the arid wastes of western Colorado.

I landed for supplies at McCoy and continued downstream until dark, camping on a sandbar near the mouth of Catamount Creek. While the fire flickered and the crescent moon sank over the river, a lonesome cowboy rode along the opposite shore singing "Can I Sleep in Your Barn Tonight, Mister?" The sights of the day seemed to pass in review: waves crashing on the forward deck, sections of the riverbank gliding by, sunlight shining through clear green swells, and rocks that the boat had skimmed whizzing past with trails of foam in their wakes. It was a traveling man's dream come true.

The *Rob Roy*'s course the next morning gave frequent glimpses of construction work along the Dotsero cutoff. Resuming my free ride on the endless belt of the Colorado, I came to a drop where the river was engorged by the new railroad embankment on the right. The constricted channel broke into a foaming rapid among jagged rocks. I made a rough passage of it, getting my first soaking early in the day. The second came just around the next bend in a savage succession of waves. The weather was glorious, though, and my sodden clothes dried rapidly.

The *Rob Roy* passed construction sites all morning until I became accustomed to the whine of power shovels and the chatter of grading machines. The boom of blasting shots echoed up and down the valley. Drillers worked on a cliff face high over the river, slung in bosun's chairs.

It was easy going to the hamlet of Burns. Landing for supplies at the bridge, I walked into a new bar and dance hall called the Oasis. While I was buying food among the stacks of empty beer cases, the proprietor asked where I was heading, taking me for a job hunter.

"Why," I said, "I'm going down the river and shoot some rapids."

"Shoot some what?" He eyed me suspiciously. "Ain't no rabbits left in this country, and besides, where's your gun?"

After embarking again I entered a winding labyrinth called Rouge Canyon, the longest one I had seen. This is the first canyon along the Colorado with the horizontal lines that are characteristic of the Grand Canyon region, the result of river erosion through level beds of sedimentary rock. The hard rock layers break off sharply to form vertical cliffs and the softer layers form gentle slopes. There was more vegetation in Rouge Canyon than in the Grand Canyon region, however; occasional pines and firs rose along the riverbank and the upper slopes were dotted with cedars.

The boat splashed through some fast stretches in the upper canyon and at noon reached Red Dirt Creek Rapids, a 250-yard run among large, submerged rocks. Ordinarily this would require no great care, but it looked treacherous because of a temporary wooden bridge across the main channel. I landed and decided to run through one of the spans in the center of the current. Since the bridge was already in the whitewater it took some careful steering to guide the boat through the narrow opening. I ducked under the bridge safely and then curved between two submerged rocks and rode the lower waves, feeling well satisfied with the boat when she bounced through untouched.

Below the construction work the valley reverted to a semi-wilderness. Glad to be away from roaring trucks and cement mixers, I ate lunch on a secluded sandbar. On leaving Rouge Canyon at 3:00, the boat entered a

This photograph of Glenwood Canyon shows what Hal referred to as "a nasty fall" about a mile below the power plant. He nearly swamped his boat there.

Cottonwood Falls in Glenwood Canyon on the Colorado River in Garfield County, Colorado. The river drops roughly one hundred feet per mile in this stretch.

There were many small farms in Glenwood Canyon when Hal paddled through in 1933.

wide valley flanked by high yellow hills and cliffs. A flock of ducks beat the water into foam, great blue herons waded along shore, magpies fluttered under the cliffs in their contrasting plumage of black and white, and a few hawks and eagles soared over the bluffs.

At Sweetwater Creek, the only tunnel on the cutoff was approaching completion. The rails had already been laid from Dotsero to the downstream portal. Around the next bend stood boxcars and locomotives. Work trains lined the tracks, housing gandy dancers who were laying the steel. Their wives and children worked in little garden patches along the tracks.

The boat slapped along through easy riffles the rest of the afternoon until I reached the Dotsero bridge at suppertime, having cruised thirty miles since morning. The local postmistress and her husband, Doc Yost, made me comfortable in a log cabin behind the post office. I cooked supper in the cabin and then joined the evening circle in the post office lobby, which also happened to be Mrs. Yost's best sitting room.

Doc told us about his early adventures in the Rockies, when he had run the mail stage to Leadville in the eighties and when he was a young cowhand seeking his fortune in the Rouge Canyon country. Forty years before, he had made a rafting voyage from Burns to Dotsero with irrigation pipe. His remaining hopes for prosperity depended on the Dotsero cutoff, since

By 1933, there were already several hotels in Glenwood Springs, where tourists took advantage of the hot springs.

he had been waiting forty years for the town to amount to something.

The next morning I took aboard the first passenger on my trip: George Yost, Doc's little boy, who rode a mile or so to the mouth of the Eagle River. Then I paddled for miles through a quiet section of Glenwood Canyon, descending only two sharp pitches. Soon I reached the dead water behind the Shoshone Dam and it took me the rest of the morning to paddle against a headwind to the dam itself, beneath magnificent walls that rose two thousand feet above the river.

The stretch of two and a half miles below the dam would be difficult to navigate, since the river drops a hundred feet per mile. As Wallace Stegner wrote about Sam Adams's belief that it would be easy to cruise the river from the foot of Gore Canyon to the sea,

> The "prosperous voyage" from which he reluctantly turned away would have included stretches like the rapids along which Highway 50 now runs near Glenwood Springs. Anyone can drive it at any time during the spring runoff and test himself by imagining what it would be to put a boat or raft through that wildhorse current with its twenty-foot waves.[1]

From the high concrete dam a large part of the river flows through a tunnel

Hal Leich and the *Rob Roy* departed peaceful Glenwood Springs, Colorado, to continue down the Colorado River.

several miles to the Shoshone power plant. I hailed a trucker from Wyoming, who carried my outfit to the power plant for fifty cents.

I decided to try the run from the power plant despite warnings from the engineers, who told me about some more bad rapids ahead. I slid *Rob Roy* off the lawn of the turbine house at 1:30 at the spot where Ellsworth Kolb and Bert Loper began their voyage a number of years before. I crossed the river just above the tunnel outlet and landed to look over the rapids. The first mile below the plant drops fifty feet, and the second one forty. Since the flow was greater than in Byers Canyon, I realized I would not have an easy passage.

The first three-quarters of a mile gave the boat some fast, rough going. There were no rocks in the channel, but heavy waves pounded her decks, flooded over the spray cover, and dashed up on my clothes. I took it all without bothering to land until I went over a small fall that gave me a real surprise. The drop was not more than three feet, but the suddenness of sinking over the edge gave me a curious feeling. The bow sank into boiling water, the spray cover sagged, and *Rob Roy* wallowed down the outrun half full of water. Steering her through the succeeding wave troughs with that weight of water in her belly took all my strength on the paddle. I welcomed a quieter stretch that gave me a chance to bring her ashore and bail her out with my hat.

A mile below the power plant the entire river plunged through a rocky chute, breaking into five or six foaming haystacks. After the near-disaster at the fall, I landed and looked the place over carefully. But in starting through I did not give the boat enough room to swing into the proper channel. *Rob Roy* made a port entrance and drifted diagonally into the worst of the waves. Luckily a sidewinder swung her around end-first before she reached the heavy water; otherwise it would have gone hard with her—and me. Halfway through I jumped for a line of rocks in the middle of the channel and held the boat by the stern line while I tried to collect my wits. Then I hauled her close to the rocks and jumped aboard again. The rest was easy since I had the boat under control. "Well begun is half done" applies nowhere more aptly than in shooting river rapids, as I discovered on several occasions.

Another fast, rocky descent began a hundred yards down the river. I made this easily on the left side, sluicing down a small flume through the fall, scraping rocks once or twice, and riding the lower waves buoyantly. The rest of the river to Glenwood Springs was splendid going—fast, rough, and rock-free, with the apex of the current racing through a series of curling wave crests.

Hal completing emergency boat repairs below Glenwood Springs.

Hal recorded this photograph as showing the Book Cliffs, located between Glenwood Springs and Grand Junction, Colorado. He indicates the Colorado River is exactly one mile above sea level at this spot.

At the mouth of No-Name Creek, a crowd of bathers helped me careen the boat to empty the water and then they swam alongside for a few yards until she started into the next rapid. A swift ride in the shadow of a high wall brought her around Tunnel Point, at the lower end of Glenwood Canyon, and then she rode down a sunny river between rows of tall poplars at Glenwood Springs amid the fumes of the hot sulphur springs that have made the town famous.

While several small boys watched my boat, I located a room at the Glenwood Hotel. The porter and I carried the boat, still loaded, through the main street to the hotel, where I saw her safely docked in the sample room. I was pleased that my little ship had come through so well, even though she was now a patchwork of twine, rawhide, and adhesive tape, and I was confident that she could carry me to Grand Junction—another hundred miles and as far as I had ever planned to take her.

The next morning I found out at the Glenwood post office about the paddler who had given Hot Sulphur Springs its first view of a folding kayak. He was Herr Peppo Saeckler, a German *sportler* who called himself "the world's champion canoe paddler." He began his journey on the Fraser River, but how far he got down the Colorado I was never able to learn. One record at least that he claimed will stand for a long time to come: during a spring flood he once paddled from Dayton down the Miami River to the Ohio and then to Louisville—three hundred miles in one day!

Herr Peppo was not the first person to use a collapsible rubber boat on a western river. In 1842 Lt. John C. Fremont carried a folding rubber boat on his first expedition through the Rockies, using it for fording streams. On returning east after exploring the Wind River Range in Wyoming, he floated down the North Platte, barely escaping disaster in what is now called Fremont Canyon.

The weekend in Glenwood Springs passed luxuriously. I slept late, ate many stacks of hotcakes at the Owl Café, and swam in the hot springs pool, the largest in the world. The observer at the U.S. Geological Survey's stream gauging station told me that the river was at a normal summer stage. He spoke of the fury of the spring floods, and of what happened to anyone unfortunate enough to fall in below Shoshone Dam during high water.

The most spectacular sight in Glenwood Springs was the departure of huge articulated freight locomotives as they highballed out of the yards in tandem and gathered speed for the upriver trip, pulling eighty or ninety cars. Roaring as their wheels slipped on the shiny rails, they shook the ground near the waterfront while dozens of hoboes ran alongside and tried to swing themselves aboard.

The Colorado River lived up to its name on Monday morning when I left Glenwood Springs—it was a deep red because of heavy rain the day before. The boat sailed under the railroad bridge and passed the mouth of the Roaring Fork, which was still clear and green. I had bought a Denver newspaper that morning, but in a few minutes its lurid pages melted into pulp when *Rob Roy* pounded through heavy waves in a continuous succession of fast, hard riffles. Since there was no profile map of the river from Glenwood Springs to Grand Junction, I could not tell what the descent would be, but I soon found that it was high for the first six miles.

The river flowed through a winding, V-shaped trough, and in almost every hundred yards it entered a stretch of fast, broken water. Soon after lunch I hit the last of the heavy water—or rather, the water hit me. Her bow dipped into a high-crested wave below a fall, nosed hundreds of pounds of water onto the forward deck, and slowly emerged with the canvas deck sagging.

Ashore for an inspection, I found that the forward frame, already cracked in Gore Canyon, had broken off in three places. Another longitudinal had snapped off, too. It took me more than two hours to dismantle the boat, repair her with oak splints and twine, and put her together again stronger than ever.

On reembarking I entered a quieter stretch and one that was more settled than the upper river. The valley widened and the gradient decreased until I was troubled again with a flat river, like a delta, that split into many braided channels. Near the bridge at Silt I counted eleven branches. Although I always tried to choose the larger branch, I was soon cruising down a runnel no bigger than a gutter. Eventually I was stranded on a damp gravel bar far above the main channel and had to drag the boat down a bank into the reassembled river.

I landed near the town of Antlers in the early evening to find a campsite. Nearby I met a young rancher irrigating a sugar beet patch, who introduced himself as Chuck Everett. I knew we would get along from the keen interest he showed in the *Rob Roy*, and my liking increased when he told me his favorite sport was swimming down the Colorado riffles at high water. After supper at his father's house, we sat around the table for several hours visiting with neighboring ranchers. I slept in an empty potato cellar near the river, well protected from a heavy rain.

Chuck called me at 6:00 the next morning for a fine breakfast of pancakes and homemade jelly. Chuck and his father talked for an hour afterwards about prospecting down the river. They advised me to carry a gold pan on my travels, saying there was placer gold in the sandbars below Moab. I finally shoved away at 8:15.

After the rainstorm the weather was overcast and cool—ideal for exertion. As I passed downstream the clouds broke to reveal a wide view over Cactus Valley, the broad irrigated land on which the Everett ranch was located, between the Grand Hogback and the eastern face of the Book Cliffs, a bold escarpment that loomed ahead.

The muddy current and floating driftwood already showed the effects of the rainstorm. All day *Rob Roy* sped down a swift river below the abutment of the Book Cliffs, which rise in a mighty escarpment 3,500 feet above the northern shore. Streamers of storm clouds gradually cleared to show the carved, eroded walls rising to impressive summits. According to the ranchers, the Book Cliffs were so named because the capes along the river looked like a row of books on a gigantic shelf. Major Powell, on the other hand, said the formation got its name from the minute horizontal rock stratification, since the thin layers looked like the pages of a book. The Book Cliffs extend for a hundred miles north of the river in Colorado and Utah and provide an estimated reserve of 400 billion barrels of oil in its beds of shale. Some pieces of this rock are so rich in oil that they burn like a dry log. The early Mormon settlers distilled oil from shale until a cheaper supply of oil was discovered in Pennsylvania in 1859.

Somewhere below the settlement of Rifle, the river cut across the mile-high contour line and I realized that I had already dropped more than three thousand feet from Grand Lake. At Parachute Creek I took two hours for lunch under some willows. The town of Grand Valley nearby is a reminder that the Upper Colorado, above the mouth of the Green River, was long known as the Grand River, and many other names offer similar evidence: Grand Lake, the Grand Hogback, Grand Mesa, and Grand Junction. After years of dispute the name was changed to the Colorado River by a joint resolution of Congress on July 25, 1921, in answer to those who claimed that the Green River was the principal tributary of the great stream that had carved the Grand Canyon. Yet hydrologists still refer to it as the Upper Colorado to distinguish it from the real thing.

During the afternoon the boat weathered four or five hard rapids, with savage waves but no rocks. The increased volume of water caused higher, heavier waves, but the boulders were well submerged. After the delightful green and white waves of the headwaters, it seemed strange to see reddish foam in the rapids. The riffles looked like newly plowed fields of earth, with red spray spurting incongruously from each hillock.

Below these stretches of heavy water the river seemed to boil. Great surges like fountains rose under the boat, twisting her off her course. Whirlpools, eddies, and powerful sucking backwaters wrenched her framework until she squeaked and groaned under the strain. Then I would come to another drop where the river fell below the level of my eyes, like coming to the end of the world, where the sea was supposed to drop off into space, or like sailing down to the brink of Niagara Falls. Sometimes I could see the rapids ahead by standing and balancing uneasily on the keel framework. If the drop were still too steep to be seen, I would put ashore before being sucked into the rough water. Several times I tried poising on the very tongue of a rapid, backpaddling madly while trying to pick the best channel, but this was not a sound idea in really dangerous water.

After stopping at De Beque for supplies, I camped on a gravel bar three miles below town. The fast current and steady work at the paddle enabled *Rob Roy* to log 40 miles for the day, despite two hours for lunch. She had dropped 570 feet in elevation, an average descent of nearly 15 feet per mile.

Below Glenwood Springs good drinking water was becoming scarce. The muddy current was not appealing and the pollution load added a health hazard that had not been present on the upper river. I was lucky to find a pool of clear water in the gravel bar near the camp.

One of the delights of cruising western rivers is the abundance of dry driftwood. There is no tedious splitting of wood that one must often do in the damp eastern woods. I piled up a great heap of driftwood, set it ablaze, and cooked a good corn chowder while the half-moon sailed over the river.

Most of the next morning I paddled through still water and before noon entered the walls of De Beque Canyon, or Hogback Canyon as it is sometimes called, a shallow serpentine gorge with water-worn caves high on the yellow rock sides. The sluggish current meandered among sandbars from one vertical wall to the other. Back in the Midwest the canyon would be a state park with college boys guiding tourists through "the lemon squeezer," "the devil's punch bowl," and "fat man's misery." In Colorado it is unnoticed.

Halfway through the canyon I saw a large deer on a low, grassy island. It ducked into the brush when I passed. A man who was building a log cabin of discarded railroad ties a short distance downstream told me that the deer had lived on the island ever since it was a fawn.

I reached the High Line irrigation dam at Cameo shortly after noon. This concrete dam is equipped with a roller crest of metal that can be adjusted according to the river stage. During a flood the river would cover the railroad track if the crest could not be lowered. It diverts water into the fifty-five-mile High Line Canal, which irrigates the prosperous Grand Valley peach-growing land between Cameo and Grand Junction. At one point, part of the canal's flow is siphoned under the Colorado in a tunnel nine feet in diameter.

Johnnie and Archie Carver, sons of the superintendent, told me that the best place for carrying around the dam was on the left-hand side. They crossed the river on a catwalk above the dam and helped me carry the boat. We lowered her over a steep embankment at the head of a rapid that received a good impetus from the fourteen-foot spillway of the dam.

Johnnie and Archie remembered Herr Peppo well—he was almost a legendary figure on the river. They said he had taken his boat by truck to a canal spillway about half a mile downstream.

I ran the fast water without difficulty and then stopped on a sandbar for a frugal lunch of bread and cheese. Then I came to an old concrete irrigation dam about six feet high. I felt tempted to run over the top in the empty boat until I saw how a large log, trapped in a water pocket at the foot of the dam, was being sucked under the fall repeatedly. A large wave rolled back into the fall, and I had no desire to try out *Rob Roy* under that descending weight of water. In an unusual display of good judgment, I carried the boat around on the left bank. With the help of some fishermen I lifted her over a barbed wire fence and set her afloat below the dam. They cautioned me about the rock-strewn rapid below, but the boat came through with her decks dry.

One more dam lay across my path: the original Grand Valley weir below the town of Palisade, with a low, wooden structure broken down near the center. *Rob Roy* ran the break beautifully in a fast flume and found herself in quiet water for the rest of the day.

West of Palisade the towering buttresses of the Book Cliffs receded from the north bank, leaving a broad bench used for peach orchards and truck farms. On the south bank a similar bench was under intensive cultivation. Ironically enough in this semi-arid region, much of the best orchard land had been ruined by too much water. Large-scale irrigation started in Grand Valley in 1883, and in the intervening years careless husbandry had allowed the soil to become "seeped," or saturated until it was swampy. So the harassed fruit growers stopped making irrigation ditches and dug a few drainage ditches instead. For miles along the southern shore I could trace a section of seeped strata in a low cliff under Orchard Mesa, where a wet band glistened between two bands of dry rock.

On my left I had occasional glimpses of the Grand Mesa, a verdant island rising far above the brown, dry valley. Its tremendous bulk rose five thousand feet above the river to a summit plateau that enjoys abundant rainfall and holds innumerable lakelets among dense forests.

I had a pleasant loaf along the lazy river, drifting along until evening watching the ducks and the great blue herons. Just above Clifton I camped in a cottonwood grove along a low clay shore. The only drinking water I could find was a trickle of irrigation seep with a strong alkaline taste. I cooked supper and watched the Book Cliffs across the river become a deep red at sunset. After a meal of canned beef and spaghetti I settled down to enjoy a last campfire before Grand Junction, where I planned to build a heavier successor to the *Rob Roy*.

It was 11:00 by the time I shoved off the next morning, but there was no hurry, since Grand Junction lay only ten miles down the valley. When I stopped for a drink of good water above the Clifton bridge, the rancher told me about an accident that had happened a few months before. A truck loaded with nine people had stalled on a hill at the Clifton bridge and rolled backwards into the river, and four of the party had drowned. Almost every year between ten to twenty people drowned in the river between Glenwood Springs and Grand Junction. This explained the terror with which the river was regarded by many of the people I talked to.

Below the river I found something I had been eager to see since my days on the Yellowstone: a nest of the great blue heron. Several were built in a cottonwood grove on the riverbank. Made of sticks in forks about twenty feet off the ground, they looked almost like driftwood caught in the branches during high water. Six or seven herons, lined along the bank, solemnly watched my progress down the river and formed a critical jury to pass on my seamanship. Every paddle stroke was keenly appraised, and the verdict was one of pettish disapproval, for the entire jury took flight with loud squawks of disgust.

As the boat approached Grand Junction, a man shouted at me from the top of a bluff: "Hey, watcha doin' down there?"

The only possible answer was a paraphrase of Thoreau's famous reply to Emerson, "Watcha doin' up there?"

Soon *Rob Roy* reached the first bridge at Grand Junction and passed the mouth of the Gunnison, a broad river flowing in from the south. It was this river junction rather than a rail one that gave Grand Junction its name. I tied up the boat near the Main Street bridge and entrusted my baggage to some people in a house nearby while I looked for lodgings. I found a pleasant room with Mr. and Mrs. Schmidt on a broad, tree-lined avenue, and with the help of his truck I saw the boat safely moored in the backyard and her cargo stowed away aloft.

CHAPTER SIX

Swapping Horses in Midstream

GRAND JUNCTION PROVED to be an oasis of shade trees and drinking fountains in an expanse of sunbaked aridity. The size and enterprise of the town impressed me. Its population had already passed ten thousand, long before the uranium boom, and its commercial importance far exceeded its size—the town ranked as the second largest mercantile center in Colorado, serving an area of fifty thousand square miles.

I had always intended to switch from the *Rob Roy* and build a sturdy wooden boat at Grand Junction, since the town was the best outfitting center above the wilderness of the deep canyon country. On the upper river I could always count on Glenwood Springs as a possible boatyard in case *Rob Roy* came to grief. But in no case did I figure on using the kayak for the big river; its light framework would not withstand the heavy rapids of the lower canyons with the load of supplies I would have to take. A boat of far greater stamina and carrying capacity was required.

I had drawn my plans for a cataract boat many months before. Building on the experience of the Yellowstone trip, I had used shirt cardboard the winter before in Evansville to experiment with hull designs. By gluing the laundry cardboard with strips of paper and waterproofing the model with varnish I could try out different shapes in the bathtub at home, the only model basin available. Finally I settled on a double-ended design with a center cockpit protected by a high coaming. She was to be a heavy rectangular punt, thirteen feet overall and three and a half feet wide, having a deeply undercut bow and stern and both ends decked over. The double-ended feature would, in effect, give me a spare bow in case the original one smashed into too many boulders.

To finance this second stage of my canyon expedition, I had expected to find a money order waiting for me at the post office general delivery. When it did not turn up, I persuaded the Western Union man to wire my father for more money by leaving my good watch as security.

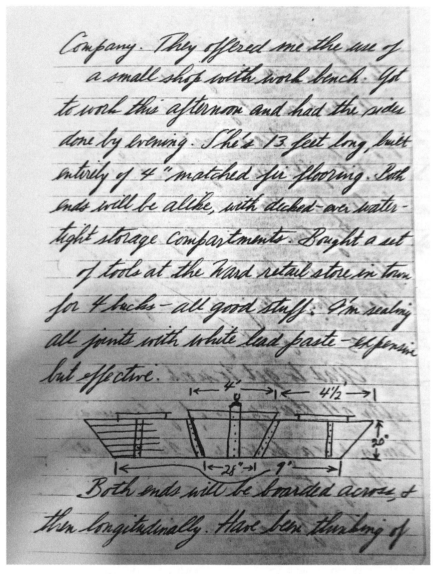

A page from Hal's river journal with a sketch of his new boat, the *Dirty Devil*, as he intended to build it.

With funds in hand, I started building the new boat at the Gibson Lumberyard the next morning. When I agreed to buy all my materials from them, they let me use an empty shed with a workbench as my boat shop. This time for four dollars I bought my own set of tools to take along as a repair kit. By nightfall I had completed the sides of the punt, building them up of matched fir flooring with white lead paste smeared along the tongue-and-groove joints. The sides were twenty inches high, with the ends trimmed off at an angle of 45 degrees, more or less. The length of the boat on deck was to be thirteen feet and the length of the bottom only nine feet because of the sharply undercut bow and stern.

That night I sent to a Denver mail-order house for two pairs of oars, one of ash and the other of fir, and a kapok life-preserver vest. Then I walked back to my room through the Saturday night crowd. Ranch hands from Utah, peach growers from Palisade, and forest rangers from the Grand Mesa gathered at the flea market that had sprung up in vacant lots along Colorado Avenue. Old gramophones, pianos, sewing machines, and parlor organs were being auctioned off, while farmers' wives sold doughnuts, huge pieces of pie, and watermelon quarters to the throng.

It is strange how ruthlessly a person will drive himself when engaged in an undertaking of his own choice. For seven straight days, beginning that Sunday, I sweated in the little shop until the boat was completed, only stopping now and then to visit a bakery for some hot doughnuts made of potato flour and honey. After lining up the sides of the boat, I covered the bottom and the ends with more of the four-inch flooring, laying the boards athwartships. Then I decked over each end for four and a half feet, leaving a four-foot cockpit amidships. I built a heavy six-inch coaming around the cockpit to keep out waves, and fitted a reversible seat that could be used for rowing when either end was serving as the bow.

Not satisfied with a single thickness of fir on the bottom and ends, I spaced four six-inch boards fore-and-aft along the bottom to serve as skids and covered both ends solidly with another layer of flooring, also laid fore-and-aft. After that she looked stout enough to ram the Rock of Gibraltar, and I gave up a vague notion about armoring her ends with sheets of steel. Her weight gave me some uneasiness, but after all, I didn't plan to tote her down a railroad track like the *Rob Roy*. To aid in lifting the boat, I ordered six iron fittings forged at a blacksmith shop and bolted them on as "hand holts," as the old canyon runners used to call them. Two went along each side and one on each end—if anything were needed to confirm her coffin-like appearance this was it.

I had planned to build a watertight compartment in each end, with hatchways through the decks, following the example of Major Powell and most of the other expeditions. But by the time I had finished sheathing the bottom and ends the boat weighed so much that I decided to forego the two bulkheads that were required. I half-excused this change in plans by noting that I could thus sleep aboard on rainy nights, as well as carry spare oars inboard.

As I got around to applying the finishing touches, I could hardly do my work without getting off to one side and admiring her great, powerful lines. She was my idea of a rough-water boat and I fell more in love with her buxom lines the more I saw of her. Her design was the essence of functional simplicity—as modernistic as tomorrow's skyscraper, without a curve in sight.

During my stay ashore, I asked several people about hazards on the lower river and was told to see Dr. A. P. Drew, the local horse doctor, who was the chief authority on the subject. One morning I stopped in at his ill-scented establishment and found him fondling a gruesome object that he identified as a horse's skull. I wouldn't have minded the specimen so much if the horse's eyes had not been in place. Telling the kindly old veterinarian that I was no judge of horse flesh, I quickly shifted the subject to the Colorado River. He stopped probing into the interior of the horse's head, wiped his hands, and eagerly took me to see his Colorado River fleet, made up of two rowboats and a canoe. It was easy to see that he was a genuine river runner, one of the few that I met. He related many an exciting tale of narrow escapes in the riffles below Grand Junction and warned me especially of the rapids in Ruby Canyon, much dreaded by Grand Junction navigators. He had been all the way down to Westwater, Utah, but had never attempted the dangerous canyon below there.

As in Livingston, word got around about my plans and several of the curious dropped in. One afternoon, as I was doing some final scraping and painting, a fellow navigator paid me a visit. He had tracked me down to see whether I would rent my new boat, since he intended to cruise into Ruby Canyon to search for dinosaur bones. I told him the yarns I had heard about Ruby Canyon, but my visitor—a middle-aged man of professorial appearance—did not seem disturbed by its evil reputation.

Adding that the boat was not for rent, I referred him to Doc Drew for assistance.

By the end of the week the oars and life preserver arrived, as well as profile maps of the river below the mouth of the Green from the U.S. Geological Survey. Another addition to my outfit was a seven-shot Smith and Wesson .22 revolver with a broken handle that I bought for $2.50 in a secondhand store.

Finally I began the last odd jobs before launching. I gave the boat a good soaking with a thin mixture of white lead, linseed oil, and turpentine, but decided to delay painting her until reaching Moab, since she would probably require repairs by that time. I also painted the packsack and duffel bag with water repellent and made floor gratings from leftover boards. The last job was to fit a new spray cover of heavy canvas that could be lashed down to some screw eyes along the decks.

The completed scow resembled an empty packing case or coffin more than a conventional boat, but she was the child of my imagination and of my own hands and I was proud of her. The question of a name for her was puzzling, until one came to mind that seemed appropriate for her peculiarities. Starvation Creek, Muddy Creek, and Stinking Spring Creek flow together in southern Utah to form the Dirty Devil River, a writhing torrent that meanders through tortuous canyons in the badlands of the "Robbers Roost" country to debouch into the Colorado at the foot of Narrow Canyon. It was after this unsavory stream that I chose, in a perverse moment, to name the product of my handiwork.

The morning of Monday, August 14, found me running around Grand Junction on last-minute errands in the hope of getting away some time that day. One annoying problem had solved itself: my punctured hand had finally healed after two weeks of changing drains. A sister at the hospital told me I was lucky that I hadn't lost it.

It was no easy task to dismantle the *Rob Roy*, since nearly every joint was bound with twine and some of the water-soaked ribs had swollen in the brass ferrules. I was surprised how the staunch little vessel collapsed into bundles like a pup tent. With the dismembered kayak on my back, I made a last portage down Colorado Avenue to Mr. Schmidt's storage warehouse, where my faithful water bronco found a resting place.

At 3:00 the company truck was available. Before leaving we placed the *Dirty Devil* on the lumberyard scales and found that she weighed 405 pounds with oars and fittings. I could still lift one end with one hand—not without some grunting—but I knew that her weight would increase when she began soaking up water. The die was cast—I had made the irrevocable choice between ruggedness of construction and lightness of weight.

My bill at the lumberyard was thirty-five dollars, exactly what I had estimated more than a year before. I rode in the back of the truck with the boat and two skeptical yard hands who were curious to see her in the water. It took the four of us to slide the boat down a gravel bank on the far side of the Main Street bridge. The *Dirty Devil* began leaking fast, but in a few minutes the wood swelled and the seams started to close.

In trying her out I was startled to find that the oar blades would barely reach the water. The rowlocks were two feet above the surface because of the high freeboard, and my seven-foot oars were not long enough to bite into the water effectively. But soon the rowlocks wore into the shafts of the oars a little, allowing the blades to dip in more. After the speedy *Rob Roy* the slow gait of the *Dirty Devil* was disappointing, but she was much easier to steer accurately. I bailed her out, loaded my camping outfit, food, and box of tools, waved to my helpers, and sailed from Grand Junction at 4:30.

The evening's run of ten miles did not give the *Dirty Devil* a real test, since she encountered nothing more exciting than mild riffles over gravel bars. The scenery was beautiful at sunset; in the east I had a glimpse of the Grand Mesa hovering on the skyline, and ten miles to the north the headlands of the Little Book Cliffs marched in serried rank. To the south pinnacles of the Uncompahgre Plateau rose four thousand feet above the river, their red summits gleaming in the sunset.

I camped on a sandy bank that evening across from some undercut cliffs. My camping outfit was down to a minimum and did not even include a tent. In the arid region I was entering there was little use for one anyway, and I carried a green tarpaulin to spread over my blanket when the night was threatening. To provide drinking water I had bought a galvanized bucket and a gallon insulated jug. Before rolling in for the night I filled the bucket with muddy river water. By morning most of the sediment had settled to the bottom and the rapid evaporation had cooled it off considerably. I carefully drained off the clear water on top into the jug and kept it in the shade below deck. This provided clear, fairly cool water during the heat of midday, although its purity was not improved in the slightest.

Horsethief Canyon on the Colorado River is located near the Colorado-Utah border.

The next morning when the boat had drifted into a secluded stretch, I stripped off my clothes and swam alongside for a while. The solid platforms of the decks allowed me to sunbathe or dive, pleasures that had not been possible on the flimsy decks of the kayak. Late in the morning I passed the last ranch house before the entrance to Horsethief Canyon. The railroad and the highway curved far away to the north; here the river entered the wildest region that it had so far traversed below its source.

The canyon is a twisting gorge formed by the Colorado River slicing into a section of the Uncompahgre Plateau. The vertical walls, several hundred feet high, are of reddish sandstone, curiously waterworn by ancient floods. It is typical of the "rimrock" country, the land of high, barren plateaus broken by deep, vertical canyons, with the upper layer of resistant rock forming a clean-cut rim along the tops of the canyons. Horsethief Canyon is notable chiefly for the small attractive glens along its walls. Tributary streams have carved out bowl-shaped amphitheaters, some of them extending a hundred yards into the solid rock. The floors of these glens are carpeted with grasses and shrubs, and the overhanging rock walls are moistened by the dripping waters of the tributaries.

There was not even a riffle in the canyon. The boat provided enough room for me to stretch out and enjoy lunch onboard and the current carried me a mile or so while I rested from rowing. Soon I came to a hairpin bend where the river ended its northwesterly course from Grand Junction and began a southwesterly trend, which it followed most of the way across southern Utah. At the apex of the bend, the railroad came into the canyon through a tunnel after a wide detour.

Late in the afternoon I entered Ruby Canyon, decorated with turrets and pinnacles on its three-hundred-foot walls, so named because of the deeply colored red rock through which it cuts. Below the tiny station of Shale, I saw the first person I had met since the afternoon before: an Italian section hand who was fishing alongshore. At my appearance he began shouting in broken English and waving his arms downstream. I finally gathered that another boat had passed him only a short while before. If this was the case, I could understand his amazement at seeing two boats on the lonely stream in one afternoon.

I kept at the oars and soon reached the next bend, a right-angled curve to the south in a narrow canyon. The river fell away into a stretch of broken water caused by an outcrop of black, polished granite along the canyon floor. Close inshore was the other boat, a heavily laden open skiff that I recognized as the flagship of Doc Drew's navy. She was the only boat besides my own that I actually saw afloat anywhere on the river.

On the rocky shore stood my dinosaur-hunting acquaintance, holding the skiff by a line. His companion, waist-deep in the swift current, guided the vessel around some jagged rocks. The river broke into a rapid among rocky islets, curving around the sharp bend in two channels. Although the *Dirty Devil* was entering the first real rapid that she had tried, and though several inches of bilge water sloshed around from the day's leakage, I let her whoop down into the outer channel without landing to look it over. Standing upright in the cockpit, I had a clear view of the water ahead while I rowed slowly against the current in order to steer and check her speed. The waves were not alarming, but the channel, winding among the rocks, required careful steering. I used the same technique that had worked so well on the Yellowstone and kept perfect control all the way through, even though the oars were a little short. Below the rough water I tied up and walked back to the place where the boneseekers were still toiling with their craft.

As I approached, they guided their boat safely through the lower end of the rapid and moored alongshore. Considering her heavy load and open hull, it was remarkable that they had been able to line her through at all.

They could not report anything startling in the way of dinosaur bones, but said there were signs of gold in the area. Actually the golden clouds of sunset above us were the only rewards we were likely to get out of the voyage. An account of their hardships appeared in the *Grand Junction Sentinel* on August 20:

> Two well known local men, a geologist and an artist, returned to this city Thursday night after a thrilling and hazardous voyage of 50 miles on the Colorado River. . . . This perilous trip was made in a small 14-foot boat made of celotex and metal. . . . Many and varied were the experiences reported by the two men while traveling Horsethief and Ruby Canyons. They reported that many of the most dangerous places in the river were shallow channels that looked very safe from the bank. Here the speed of the water was greater, they said, and as a result of low water more boulders were exposed, which constantly threatened the safety of the voyagers and their craft. . . . An inexperienced river man would certainly meet disaster on this river. Waves sometimes four feet high, whirlpools, and side currents, all contribute to the hazards of the voyage. . . . In many places, the men reported, they were forced to let the boat down the canyon on lines. Their feet were wet from morning to night.

What was a voyage to remember in their flimsy, overloaded skiff had proved easy going for my decked cataract boat.

The geologist suggested that I meet them at a cabin a short distance below Ruby Canyon. While I continued down the river, they examined the granite ledge across the riverbed. This formation extended downstream almost half a mile and had been cut by water action into intricate passageways. I enjoyed riding the swift current through narrow channels that wound between huge blocks of gleaming rock, worn into strange grooves, ridges, and potholes.

I never did see the cabin and kept on down the river until long after sunset. Intent on spending the night in Utah, I rowed steadily to the deserted railroad station of Utaline. Just after crossing the state line, the boat grounded on a sandbar in the twilight. Freeing her again was a far different matter from pushing off a kayak—I had to strain to ease her over the bar. This welcome to the state of Utah did not seem at all propitious.

I made a good camp on the right bank under some cottonwoods. Thirty miles of hard rowing through mostly still water left me no energy for mooning around the campfire. I cooked some pork and beans and rolled into bed early, to the howling of a band of coyotes in the hills half a mile from the river. Coyotes do not attack an able-bodied person, but it was reassuring nevertheless to have the old seven-shooter under my pillow.

Just before going to sleep I glanced at a dark mountain mass silhouetted against the starry northern sky. Suddenly a pale gleam shimmered against the blank rock wall. The tremulous glimmer faded for a moment, then reappeared, more brightly. Every moment it seemed to increase in intensity. Five or six minutes later I heard an approaching freight locomotive, miles down the river, the headlight of which caused the gleam.

CHAPTER SEVEN

Ulysses (Junior Grade)

T HE OTHER BOAT PASSED down the river early the next morning and had gone around the bend by the time I pushed off. The morning went rapidly while I rowed steadily down the quiet current. Much of the time I stayed in the shade of magnificent cottonwoods along the southern shore, grateful for relief from the intense sunshine and the hot, dry wind that blew off the barren hills. Shortly before noon I saw the water tank of the railroad at Westwater and pulled into a landing on a sandy beach by Doc Drew's flagship.

"Where you figurin' on going on that boat, son?" a grizzled rancher asked me as I pulled alongshore.

"Down the river as far as she'll go."

"Do you know what's ahead of you around the next bend?"

"Well, I can get a faint idea from the river profile maps. They show a drop of twenty-eight feet to the mile in Westwater Canyon."

"Maybe so. But they don't tell you that only one boat has gone through whole, and that she was manned by a couple of the toughest river rats on the Colorado."

"You mean Kolb and Loper?"

The rancher nodded. "If you've got a minute, I can show you some things up at the house you'll be interested in."

The rancher, E. C. Malin, dried off the windshield of his car, although why anyone would use Colorado River water to wash anything was a mystery. We drove half a mile into town, a collection of frame buildings near the Denver and Rio Grande water tank. Malin's stepfather, deputy sheriff at the time, had helped Ellsworth Kolb and Bert Loper on their memorable voyage through the canyon a number of years before. They had spent two days in the canyon, taking movies and having many narrow escapes in the cataracts.

In his parlor Malin showed me a treasured copy of Kolb's book, *Through the Grand Canyon from Wyoming to Mexico*. A yellowed clipping from the *Grand Junction Daily Sentinel* gave a spirited description of his voyage and quoted Kolb as rating the rapids of Westwater Canyon more dangerous than any on the lower river, either in Cataract Canyon or in the Grand Canyon itself. I reflected that Ellsworth Kolb, of all men, should know.[1]

Malin warned me about a bad whirlpool halfway through the canyon and wished me luck at the riverbank. I felt grateful for his kindness, since I had not been aware that Westwater Canyon is one of the most formidable in the entire Colorado River basin. The river profiles had given me the impression that it would be like Blacktail Canyon or Red Gorge, though with heavier rapids because of the greater flow of water. I began to understand, however, that the *Dirty Devil*—and her skipper too—were about to undergo a rigorous test. Except for the shortness of the oars—and I could do nothing about them at the time—the boat was ready for anything. I decided to try to get through the canyon by nightfall.

Embarking at noon, I ate a light lunch while floating downstream toward the wide canyon entrance. An odd feeling swept over me as a freight

Cottonwood trees line the Colorado River above Westwater Canyon, Grand County, Utah.

train headed upriver, her hoboes waving and yelling at the little boat. That was the last bit of steel rail to approach the Colorado all the way down to Needles, California, four hundred miles to the southwest. I was cutting another tie with my fellow men.

I passed the mouth of the Little Dolores River, flowing in from the south, just before the boat swung into the bend at the canyon's head. On the right bank of the Colorado a sheer sandstone cliff, many hundreds of feet high, rose from a jumble of rock along the river. At the canyon's entrance the boat sailed through a short rapid, caused—like the one in Ruby Canyon—by an outcrop of dark, polished granite. Although the punt hit one or two small rocks, hidden under the yellow foam, she responded nicely to the slightest movement of the oars and picked her way safely among the ledges.

Inside Westwater Canyon the Colorado burrows deeply into the hard, underlying rock structure. Slowly the steep V-shaped inner trough deepens until the gleaming black walls, nearly vertical on both sides, rise more than a hundred feet above the river. A wide bench extends on either side of the inner gorge to the base of the sandstone walls that rise in sheer cliffs to the rim of the plateau. At two places the upper walls are broken so that trails can reach the river: at a widening in the river called the Little Hole shortly below the entrance, and at a large opening called the Big Hole in the lower end of the canyon.

Geologically, Westwater Canyon is a pocket edition of the Grand Canyon, the inner trough corresponding to the Granite Gorge. In both places the river has bitten through upper layers of soft sedimentary rock, deposited on the ocean floor millions of years ago, and has then cut into denser igneous rock of much greater age. This resistant formation causes very abrupt rapids, since it does not wear away into a smooth, even gradient as does a weaker rock structure.

Now the inner walls narrowed until they were not more than fifteen or twenty feet apart, rising from the water without leaving a shore where a man could stand. Between steep black walls the river churned and swirled, flowing furiously through two strong rapids. The *Dirty Devil* sailed through both of them without the spray cover, since I could tell from the map that the worst water would come below the Little Hole. She splashed along on an even keel, thumping into the waves with her blunt undercut bow and easily surmounting them. Then the gradient slackened and she entered smooth water at the Little Hole. I landed on a sandy beach to check my gear and look around. Many deer tracks came down to the smooth pool from a ravine that led up into a break in the wall.

After bailing out and fitting the spray cover tightly, I pushed off downstream at 2:00. At first the river was disappointing. The map showed a decided drop just below the Little Hole, but for the first half mile there was only a moderate current, until I wondered what had happened to the mighty Colorado.

It did not take long to find out. Around the next bend roared a rapid worse than any I had ever tried, far surpassing anything in Byers Canyon or in the stretch below the Shoshone power plant. Knowing how a folding kayak would nose under the overlapping breakers that rose ahead, I approached the place with caution. There was no time to land and inspect the channel; the current drew the boat down the tongue of the rapid, between steep walls, and into one large wave after another. The punt sailed through superbly when I held her back with the oars. Bucking and swaying, she rode buoyantly to the foot of the drop, her bluff bow rising easily over the steepest of the breakers.

Below the rapid I landed on a ledge to catch my breath and see how the boat had weathered it. She had taken a little water aboard, probably through the upper seams along her sides, which were not fully watertight. Otherwise everything was shipshape.

A view of Westwater Canyon taken from the Colorado River, looking upstream from Little Hole.

With increasing confidence I continued down the canyon, feeling that the boat had met her first difficult test successfully. But the fury of the river still lay ahead. One after another the cataracts came. After the first drop below the Little Hole there was no possible way to turn back or climb out—there was nothing to do but plunge ahead.

Things happened so fast that I could not have given a detailed account of the rapids the next day. Time after time the *Dirty Devil* approached bottlenecks in the chasm where the river disappeared in a smother of foam. Sometimes I could tie up the boat safely and make a precarious way along polished slanting walls to take a look ahead. Sometimes the swift current made this impossible, or the walls came down sheer on either side so I could not land. Usually it made no difference, since the gorge was so narrow that there was little choice but to take to the center, glide down on the tongue of the cataract, and try to keep her bow pointed into the waves.

The *Dirty Devil* justified all my hopes for her as a rough-water boat: she rode the waves like nothing I had ever seen before. After the first bad descents, I had full confidence in her and watched her toss and pitch in admiration. She would heave high over the first wave below the tongue and then dive into the mad turmoil of roaring surges and boiling foam, ducking her bow under one moment and lifting it high in the air the next. In nearly every cataract there was a real fall, where the river plunged over a boulder or ledge for five or six feet into a quieter pool. And every time she rose beautifully to shake the water from her decks both fore and aft and ride the lower crests.

Between the rapids lay quieter reaches one or two hundred yards long. Whenever possible I steered close to shore and tied the stern rope around a rocky projection, if I could find one, in order to rest for a moment and bail her out if necessary. She was taking some water through the spray cover opening around my waist, but even more, apparently, through open seams in her decks and topsides. I had to remove the spray cover to bail her out; then the water bucket, with one side flattened, disposed of the surplus water a lot faster than I could have done with my hat. Before pushing off again I always made sure to scoop up some river water to wet my gummy lips and quench my extraordinary thirst.

Perhaps there were a dozen first-class rapids altogether, but two of them stand out in my mind. At one spot I tied up with difficulty just above a fall that looked six or eight feet high. The whole river, confined in one narrow flume, dropped away between a large boulder on the left and a black, vertical wall on the right. I scrambled ahead on the left-hand wall, clinging to irregularities on the hard, glazed surface. I looked over the fall doubtfully, cursing myself for having tied up so close to the edge, for I would have to veer far over to the right-hand cliff to avoid a rock below the fall.

Back in the boat, I cast off and pulled furiously against the current to draw her over to the right-hand side. Then, realizing I could not make it, I straightened her out and let her slide over the edge of the fall. My heart sank when I saw the witch's cauldron below. But the *Dirty Devil* must have felt in her element, for despite a poor entrance she rode easily over the fall, bounced out of the hole at the foot, and in an instant splashed through into smoother water.

I held on to a knob with my right hand while the boat curtsied in the ripples and rubbed her side against the wall. Suddenly I became aware of the strong river smell again—the heavy, silty odor churned up in the rapids of a swift stream. To me it has always brought a sense of excitement—of unknown hazards ahead, or of a lonely campfire in a lonesome canyon. Perhaps it went back to memories of the tawny Ohio in floodtime. The Potomac, the Youghiogheny, and the Greenbrier generated the same smell at high water, and I once noticed it miles at sea off the Mississippi Delta when a spring freshet washed whole trees into the Gulf of Mexico.

The worst place in the canyon came in the middle of my course, perhaps halfway between the Little Hole and the Big Hole. I reached the head of a rapid where it was impossible to land for an inspection. From the cockpit I could see that the descent was terrifying. As she sank over the top I saw an inclined plane of angry water dropping below me, with rows of combers extending from wall to wall. It was like the moment of tension when a ski jumper leaves the takeoff and soars over the landing hill.

The boat started down the declivity bravely enough, riding everything with her usual buoyancy. A few yards down the cataract, the river made a bend to the left around a headland. And there around the corner the entire river spewed onto a huge tilted slab. The current rushed high onto the sloping surface until the force of gravity overcame the water's impetus. Half of the flow then curled back to the left and rushed down through the remaining waves of the cataract; the other half curled back to the right, swirling in a narrow pool beneath the vertical wall. It was the whirlpool about which Malin had warned me. What would happen to a voyager imprisoned in that perpetual merry-go-round I should not care to imagine.

Hal Leich standing in his newly built boat, the *Dirty Devil*, near the Cisco pump house in Westwater Canyon, Grand County, Utah.

There was only an instant to pull the boat over to the left before reaching the place where the waters parted. Since the apex of the current ran full tilt onto the sloping rock, it was impossible to avoid running the *Dirty*

Devil high onto the ledge. She struck hard, began to drop backwards, and then swung completely around—luckily to the left—plunging through the rest of the cataract stern first with her helmsman craning his neck to look at the waves ahead. How glad I was then that I had built her as a double-ender! She weathered the lower breakers and came to rest in a pool of quiet water.

From the depths of the canyon the sky seemed of the most brilliant blue, except when fleecy patches of clouds blew over the rim. The canyon sides were scoured and polished, worn by water action into curious knobs, hollows, and potholes. There was hardly a scrap of vegetation for fifty or sixty feet up the walls, showing how high the water must rise during spring floods. At such times the cataracts in the middle course of the canyon must be an awful sight indeed.

When I had recovered my composure, I pushed off again and resumed my free ride down the descending escalator of the Colorado. Soon a heavy rapid, with foam-crested rollers raging in midstream, sent showers of spray over my head and surges of solid water crashing on the decks. It was the last of the dangerous cataracts. The boat rode through several more stretches of broken water and then danced on a boiling current into the glen at the Big Hole, three hours from the Little Hole, five miles upstream. I had never spent such an exhilarating afternoon before.

There was nothing but slow water in the lower end of the canyon. I had a long, hard pull against wind and wave; my hands were heavily calloused after weeks of paddling and rowing, but they began to wear raw from the oar handles. Determined to reach the railroad pumping station near Cisco, I kept on until dark, rowing past weirdly contorted rock formations and mysterious alcoves, dim in the twilight. At last a huge monolith of sandstone on the right bank, detached from the high plateau, marked the lower gateway of the canyon.

I reached the Cisco pump house at 8:00 and found the best campsite to be right in the front yard. I built a fire near the riverbank and started cooking a belated supper when someone shouted from the other shore, asking what I was doing. In half an hour two visitors appeared: the pumping station engineer and his brother, who had been summoned by my questioner. They proved to be pleasant enough when they heard my story, though somewhat skeptical until they walked down and saw the boat for themselves. They sat around talking for a while and told me to make myself at home.

The elation that I felt that night is shown by the entry in my diary on August 16:

> I am naturally highly pleased with the Dirty Devil and her performance this afternoon. If, as Ellsworth Kolb says, Westwater Canyon is the worst place on the river, the old tub oughtn't to have so much trouble lower down, although I am not minimizing in my own mind the difficulties to be encountered between here and salt water. . . .

The optimism of four-and-twenty! I had breakfast underway the next morning when the engineer, Roscoe Hallett, arrived for the day's work. His little plant pumped water several miles overland to service steam locomotives of the Denver and Rio Grande Railroad at Cisco. While he warmed up the diesel pumper with a blowtorch, I listened to his yarns about the Colorado.

Hallett had known Westwater Canyon ever since his boyhood. He told me that Kolb and Loper had capsized three times—probably for the benefit of movie cameras on the cliffs. Their boat, a decked cedar double-ender, had lifelines along the sides, watertight compartments, and a bucket roped to each end for bailing. The boat got trapped in the whirlpool I had come across the previous day and could not escape until help arrived. Several years later two men and a woman tried the canyon in a larger boat and came to grief at the same place, where the woman was drowned in the whirlpool. I began to realize how lucky I had been in swinging to the left and not the right after coming off the tilted ledge.

In showing Hallett the river profile I learned that he had helped survey the canyon a number of years before. He questioned the accuracy of the profile, which showed a drop of only twenty-eight feet per mile. He claimed the last bad mile actually drops fifty feet. After recalling how the *Dirty Devil* had charged down those last sloping rapids, I could not dispute his contention. The surveyors may have figured the river elevations at the Little Hole and the Big Hole and then averaged the descent over five miles. Actually there are many flat sections, punctuated by terrific drops.

The only damage I could find in my outfit from the severe testing of Westwater Canyon was some rust on the set of tools. Hallett gave me some engine grease, which I smeared over the saw and plane and then I wrapped them in burlap. His parting gift was several pounds of sugar, since my supply was low. I pulled away at 10:00 and found the river hot, flat, and dull—about like the Yellowstone River below Billings. The channel curved among sandbars and mudbanks and occasionally beat against undercut clay shores. Huge logs, washed down by forgotten floods and battered to shreds in the mill of Westwater Canyon, lay stranded in the shallows while the water sucked around frayed stumps and tangled roots. Sometimes the current swept into branches of trees that had been undermined; then it took careful navigation to steer between the branches. Except for a fringe of willows and cottonwoods on the banks, there was scarcely a growing thing to be seen—rugged broken walls rose in barren terraces to an arid plateau. At one point on the left, the rimrock was broken by the side canyon of the Dolores River, which added its yellow flow to the Colorado.

A peaceful stretch of the Colorado River, looking downstream from the confluence of the Dolores River.

I kept steadily at the oars and in the afternoon passed under Dewey Bridge, the only bridge between Grand Junction and Moab. Below the bridge the river seemed to vanish into the blank wall of the Dome Plateau. After drifting nearer, I saw that the river turned south and cut directly into the high mountain mass. I rowed down the resultant canyon against a stiff upstream breeze, watching the horizontal banding of the red sandstone walls. Somewhere in this canyon was the site of another proposed dam, over one hundred feet high, which would have created the largest reservoir on the upper Colorado.

A view of the Colorado River as it runs through Professor Valley, Grand County, Utah, taken at Richardson in 1933. The La Sal Mountains are shown in the background.

Finally, at sunset, after threading the gorge for several hours, I emerged into a wide bowl called Professor Valley, surrounded by pinnacles and buttes gleaming in the sun's red rays. The effect was breathtaking after my long imprisonment between the dark walls of the canyon. It was an enchanted land of delicately molded spires, soaring temples, and turreted castles, all carved of glowing red stone. I camped on a high, sandy bank across from towering eroded cliffs whose upper crags, 2,500 feet above the river, looked as if they were forever toppling into the Colorado.

After breakfast the next morning, as I sat shooting at an empty milk can, a young beaver crawled ashore not three feet from me, sniffed the air in bewilderment, and splashed back into the river. Its ancestors of a hundred years before had lured the "mountain men" into the canyons of the Colorado basin. These early trappers like Jim Bridger and Kit Carson led a carefree life for several decades before the region was settled, roaming the valleys in search of beaver pelts in the spring, gathering for a wild rendezvous with Indian tribes in the summer, and wintering with their squaws in mountain cabins. Their knowledge of the West proved invaluable to the government exploring parties that began fanning out in midcentury under such leaders as John C. Fremont.

At the mouth of Rock Creek I came to the first rapid below Westwater Canyon. The river entered a stretch of broken water over a bed of boulders that had been washed into the main river by the creek. The current was forced over against the wall of the Dome Plateau on my right and made a wide loop beneath an undercut cliff. I let the *Dirty Devil* go slap-banging through without a look ahead. This carelessness got the boat in trouble before she was halfway through. I entered too close on the right side and was drawn closer and closer to the rocky wall until I could scarcely ply the starboard oar. Ahead a rocky cape jutted out several feet from the cliff's face. Luckily I gave one good heave on the oars in a widening of the channel and the boat shot past the cape by a hair's breadth.

The last rapid on the Upper Colorado River growled in the lower end of Professor Valley, at the mouth of Castle Creek. This small tributary had washed down a delta of large boulders, forming a dam across the main river. Over this barrier the Colorado rushed in a lively spillway. The *Dirty Devil* dipped over the edge, passed swiftly down the channel, and splashed into a series of wave crests, rolling and pitching violently. This rapid and the one at Rock Creek were forerunners of a type that became common in Cataract Canyon and the lower canyons.

Just below the quick water another deep canyon closed in on the river. A man on horseback, riding along a rough road on the narrow shore, took a couple of potshots at me with his rifle, the bullets passing at some distance overhead. I was about to reach for my seven-shooter when the current carried me around the next bend. All afternoon I pulled away for Moab, past several side canyons and around the entrenched meanders of the Big Bend. Tremendous bald domes, pyramids many hundreds of feet high, and grotesque, bulbous figures rose along the red sandstone walls. Finally the south bank opened up and I was at the highway bridge in Moab Valley, or Spanish Valley as it is called on early maps.

I tied up beside an upright slab covered by Indian picture writing, crossed the bridge, and stopped at the first ranch house, the Peterson place. The children assured me I was welcome to camp in a cottonwood grove near a wide sandbar. Two boys and a girl climbed aboard with me and piloted me to a good landing place, which I intended to use as a dry dock. The boat needed a coat of paint and I wanted to lay over in Moab anyway to make some longer oars. A fierce whirlwind swept down on us as we dragged the heavy punt onto the sandbar. We retreated into the ranch house, where the owner, Frank Peterson, asked me to stay for supper. Afterwards it rained furiously and I was offered a bed for the night.

The next morning I walked three miles up Spanish Valley to the Mormon settlement of Moab, then an obscure hamlet untouched by dreams of uranium or nuclear energy. Hemmed in by barren sandstone walls, the flat valley was a striking example of the Mormons' ability to make the desert bloom. The valley floor was covered by a variegated carpet of rich vegetation, white ranch houses appeared across verdant meadows between rows of Lombardy poplars, and clear irrigation streams carried the waters of Mill Creek through the streets of town and out along the highways.

Settlement of the valley had not come easily to the Mormons. A large, well-equipped wagon train reached the area in 1855 after arduous travel over steep terrain. The settlers built a stone fort and began irrigating the lands along Mill Creek. But their efforts to convert the Indians failed and when raiders came to burn their homes and haystacks the missionaries and farmers left, so quickly that they had no time to shut off the irrigation water. When the next Mormon group arrived several years later, the irrigation ditch had eaten down twenty-five feet into the soft soil.

After a badly needed haircut and a visit with Mr. Borman at the office of the La Sal National Forest, I arranged to work on a new pair of oars at the Bush lumberyard. For one dollar I bought a 2"x6" board of beautiful, straight-grained fir sixteen feet long, which I cut into two eight-foot lengths. Then, borrowing a rip saw, I began the task of cutting out the shafts of the oars by hand—altogether, twenty-four feet of ripping through the two-inch boards. I plied the saw most of the afternoon while a bunch of cowhands who had never seen a pair of oars before stood around giving advice.

As I was working, a fiercely mustached, sun-browned old cowpuncher named Skewes joined us. I was not surprised to learn that he was the sheriff, for he looked like a storybook character off the cover of a Wild West pulp magazine. He was not a large man but had a certain intensity and power that would command respect in any company. Skewes had ridden the country between the San Juan and Gunnison Rivers many times, through one of the wildest sections of the Old West. He had punched cattle on Pinyon Mesa, along the southeast rim of Westwater Canyon, and described the river's fury in high water, when huge logs were tossed down the rapids like twigs. He used to winter in Ruby Canyon. One spring he and two others were driving thirty-five head of cattle across some mush ice just above the rapid. Suddenly the ice cracked open and every steer went through among the jagged outcroppings. One of the men, on horseback, pulled out the critters one by one; the other two built a fire and wrapped the rescued cattle in steaming saddle blankets. Some were in the water for five hours, but they didn't lose a steer.

When the shop closed, Alfred Jorgensen, a carpenter working at the next bench, offered to let me use his shop at home the next day, a Sunday. His Scandinavian name indicated the success of the Mormons' worldwide missionary efforts. I went home with him and began shaping the oar blades with his drawknives and planes, which he sharpened for me. Back at the ranch for supper, I made a comfortable camp in the cottonwoods and held open house for eight of the nine Peterson children. The next day I finished whittling the oars and gave the punt a coat of thick white lead paint. On Monday I put on the final coat of battleship gray; she looked very handsome with her gleaming decks and topsides.

One morning the older boys at the ranch, LeGrand and Weston, took me to visit the "mummy caves" in a sandstone wilderness across the Colorado to the north. We walked half a mile up a dry, winding canyon called Courthouse Wash and scrambled up a steep wall to the east. One twenty-five-foot chimney proved to be worse than anything I had done on Longs Peak. I made it after some panting and hauled the boys up with my rope. At the top we were three hundred feet above the valley on a barren rock bench that led to a series of higher cliffs. At the base of the upper wall two shallow caves, beautifully arched, penetrated the solid red sandstone. Two flat rocks near them preserved Indian pictographs of men, mountain sheep, snakes, and bats, all clearly delineated. In one cave we found a few fragments of bone, apparently human, strewn on a sandy floor among shreds of cedar bark (in which the bodies may have been buried). It looked as if curiosity seekers had beaten trained archeologists to the site.

I became fond of the Petersons in my brief stay in Moab. Every evening the children would find an old auto tire and burn it on a low hill near the river. Then they would sing to the echoing music of my mouth organ: "The Utah Trail," "Moonlight on the River Colorado," or "Valley of the Moon." Back east songs like these had sounded vapid to my ears, but with the Colorado itself glimmering in the twilight they seemed altogether appropriate.

Then the time came to make up a grub list and buy provisions for the canyon country below Moab. For twelve dollars I bought a month's supply of food and half a dozen square quart mason jars. The white flour, corn meal, sugar, whole wheat flour, prunes, and rice I stowed in separate jars to keep them dry. The butter, cheese, ham, bacon, and canned corned beef could survive a soaking without special packing. On the last afternoon I called for my mail and felt I was getting somewhere at last when I left a forwarding address of Marble Canyon Post Office, Arizona.

The next morning I made a quick trip into town to replace a slab of bacon that some hungry dogs had raided the evening before. On the return trip I got a ride with a rancher, Mr. Parriott, who gave me four plump cantaloupes to take on my journey. One of the delights of Moab was the abundance of fresh fruit and vegetables. People often gave me watermelons, cantaloupes, tomatoes, squash, and roasting ears, all unsurpassed in size and quality. The irrigated valley was a giant hot house; protected by the surrounding walls and open to the full strength of the desert sun, it had a season of 160 days between frosts.

Most of the children were on hand to help me get underway. One by one they came down to the camp, some carrying armfuls of sweet corn, one a box of tomatoes, and another a watermelon. When everything was packed away we started across the sandbar in a caravan, each bearing a box or bag—even tow-headed little Mike, the youngest, staggered along under two pairs of oars.

After the cargo had been stowed away and the vessel brought into proper trim, I pushed off into the stream at 10:30 on Thursday, August 24. The children waved goodbye until the *Dirty Devil* disappeared around a bend. An hour of rowing in the sluggish current brought her past the mouth of Mill Creek to the canyon entrance, where the river flows southwestward out of Spanish Valley into the heart of a sandstone plateau. I left the beautiful valley with grateful memories of its inhabitants.

Below Moab the Colorado entered what was then one of the wildest, most desolate regions left in a nation of garish billboards and hotdog stands. Entrenched in places 2,500 feet below the desert plateau, the river flowed for sixty miles through a winding canyon to the Green River and then the combined waters burrowed into the rugged chasm of Cataract Canyon, a forty-mile succession of boulder-strewn cataracts. The next settlement on the river, Lee's Ferry, Arizona, lay about 280 miles from Moab.

Where Spanish Valley ended, the river flowed through a portal between rock walls some eight hundred feet high. Once within the seclusion of the canyon I stripped and plunged overboard for a swim, finding the water only three feet deep over a sandy bottom. It was fun to push the boat ahead with all my strength while holding onto the iron handle on the stern. Her weight and resulting momentum were so great that I was swept off my feet and dragged in her wake until she slowed down.

A mile below the canyon entrance an old sternwheeler lay aground on the right bank. She had once been used for supplying an oil well fifteen miles down the canyon. I thought I saw signs of life aboard, but there was no reply to my hail except a double echo from the towering walls. Several miles below, two men were washing down a gravel bank with a gasoline pump in search of placer gold. They were the last people I saw below Moab, and the popping of their little engine gradually faded into the wilderness. The rest of the day I rowed in still canyons, marveling at sheer walls rising hundreds of feet from the river, waterworn caves carved into sandstone cliffs, natural bridges of salmon-pink rock, and at flying buttresses, steep gables, thin pinnacles, and symmetrical domes.

Around midafternoon I passed the deserted oil well, perched on a terrace along the right bank. The drillers had struck oil all right, but the well caught fire and burned for weeks before it was controlled by pumping in liquid mud. When the well stopped burning the flow of oil stopped too.

Late in the day the *Dirty Devil* emerged into a short, broken valley filled with the eroded remains of red cliffs and buttes. On either shore the uplands rose to barren heights by crumbling terraces and stark headlands, piled onto one another in the wildest confusion. I camped on a sandbar twenty-one miles below Moab. For firewood I dragged a dead tree to my campsite at the water's edge and after a meal of roasting ears settled down to the pleasures of an idyllic camp. The neighboring cliffs glowed in the sunset and a crescent moon sank into the west. Here in the silent canyon came fulfillment of my recurrent desire to break away from the community of men—from conformity to white-collar traditions and the small, tiresome routines of city living.

An hour before sunrise the next morning, as I lay on my side half-asleep, a large gray owl landed with a thump on my shoulder, mistaking my angular form for a driftwood log. I could feel the grip of its talons through the woolen blanket. When my shoulder jerked under the impact it flew to the sand nearby and I had a good view of it before it soared across the river.

When I had finished bailing out the boat after breakfast, I left the bucket half-awash on shore and packed up my camping outfit. In loading the boat later, I found that the bucket had disappeared and spent fifteen useless minutes diving for it along the sandy bottom, since it might be crucial in a future swamping. Luckily I found it drifting in an eddy two miles below when I resumed the voyage.

The river coursed for miles through low sandstone canyons, but farther back from shore higher cliffs and mesas hemmed in the valley. I enjoyed the changing panorama as I swam in the sunlit current alongside the bobbing punt. Around noon I was sunning myself on the aft deck, letting her drift broadside with the oars dangling overboard, when the river gave an unexpected demonstration of its power. The downstream oar caught on the shallow bottom and the heavy iron rowlock snapped off clean. I had some extras along, but this was another lesson in how a minor lapse might endanger the success of a single-handed endeavor.

In the heat of midday the vest-pocket thermometer from my refrigeration days showed a temperature of 110 degrees in the shade. I found that I did not mind this too much. I was wearing a khaki shirt of woolen flannel and this served as insulation against the sun and the hot, dry air. Back east it would have been intolerable at 80 degrees in the usual energy-sapping humidity.

Throughout the afternoon the *Dirty Devil* swept around one curve after another beneath vertical walls of stratified rock. On the inner shore of the bend there was usually a small "bottom," or overgrown sandbar, and on the outer curve the river cut directly into the sheer red walls. Peterson told me how two prospectors had lost their boat in the ice a short distance above the Green River. Unfamiliar with the trails up on the plateau, they tried to make their way upstream by swimming across from one bottom to another. Luckily a hunting party from Moab showed them a trail across the upland.

Threatening clouds gathered over the still canyon late in the afternoon, accentuating the gloom of the rocky depths. The dark river seemed to brood on its self-inflicted captivity. Three white herons or egrets rose from the shore without a sound and flew slowly down the canyon, their pallid bodies contrasting with the somber walls. It was easy to understand why their wraith-like presence was often considered an evil omen.

A magnificent spectacle unfolded when I made my camp after rowing twenty-three miles for the day. A great square butte rose above a confusion of rock several miles north of the river. As I landed the sun broke out beneath a storm cloud. The flaming rays colored the belly of the nimbus mass and tinted the crest of the butte. Thomas Moran, painter of western canyons in the 1870s, would have delighted in the majesty of the view.

Darkness swiftly followed this vivid sunset and narrowed my vision to the circle of sandy beach in the firelight. Lightning flashes showed the *Dirty Devil* tugging at her moorings in the rising wind. I walked down to the water's edge to check the ropes while claps of thunder echoed up and down the gorge. When I returned to camp to spread my blanket under the tarpaulin I glanced at the dying fire and gasped in astonishment. The glowing coals formed in a perfect image the face of a hideous grinning devil. "Good thing I'm not superstitious," I thought, unable to turn my face from the spectacle. Shaken more than I cared to admit, I kicked sand over the embers to destroy the apparition. The storm broke loose shortly after I crawled in for the night.

Saturday was gloomy and stormy. During the morning I rowed a serpentine course down a sullen river, passing out of the broken valley into a steeper, more precipitous canyon that extended all the way to the Green River. For the first hour the great, isolated butte tapered to the sky in majestic inaccessibility. Scenes of the wildest beauty followed one another around every bend of the canyon. Incredible rock remnants soared into the clouds and sheer cliffs displayed the record of millenniums of ocean deposition. If I had wanted to get away from my fellow men I was surely succeeding.

At noon I reached the beginning of the Loop, a bowknot bend where the Colorado made a nearly perfect figure-eight design, entrenched more than a thousand feet below the rim. The river flowed eight miles to cover an airline distance of two and a half. At one spot the distance between the two meanders was only six hundred feet across an isthmus, where the vertical walls were breached until just a low heap of rubble separated the two channels. Here again was a vivid lesson in geomorphology—a prize example of Powell's theory of antecedent streams. Evidently the ancient Colorado had meandered in oxbow bends across a level plain like the lower

Mississippi, and when the whole region began to rise the river continued in its channel, cutting down as the land rose. Now it was trapped in its ancient meanders far below the original land surface.

As I entered the Loop, several violent whirlwinds—forerunners of a thundersquall—swept up the canyon like miniature tornadoes, carrying tumbleweeds three hundred feet into the air. The main storm, roaring out of the hot, rocky wilderness to the southwest (a desert breeding ground of thunderstorms), caught the *Dirty Devil* in midstream on the first loop. The wind and the waves were so furious that the boat was actually borne back upstream, pitching and tossing despite my best efforts at the oars. Then a respite allowed me to round the bend while the wind, lost in the labyrinth, went moaning around the corners of broken walls in capricious gusts. On the other side of the first loop, the full force of the storm gathered astern and the pitching boat spooked beneath high, undercut cliffs. The continuous reversal of direction had me dizzy by the time the boat escaped from the maze, in midafternoon.

Now the river took a more direct course to the southwest and the canyon walls became ever higher and more spectacular. On the right bank I passed the Slide, a huge rockslide where the whole side of the canyon had come down in a heap of fragments the size of small houses, obstructing the river halfway across its bed. There was scarcely a ripple in the constricted channel, but in high water the current must flow like a millrace.

Another thunderstorm scoured the canyon as the boat wound around some bends below the Slide. In the early evening I was surprised to reach the mouth of the Green River, flowing in from the north out of the deep gorge of Stillwater Canyon. One moment I looked ahead and saw nothing but a blank rock wall; the next I saw I was rounding a formidable headland at the lonely confluence. Where the waters mingled the two rivers seemed to be of equal size. Whether the Green or the old Grand was the true source, I was now sailing indisputably on the main Colorado River, having completed the first voyage from the headwaters to the junction.

Shortly before my trip, a Colorado River navigator wrote that fewer than one hundred men had seen this spectacle at the junction of the Green and the Colorado. True enough, no tourists yodeled beneath the pinnacles of the Land of Standing Rocks when I arrived, but it is certain that many trappers, hunters, explorers, prospectors, geologists, engineers, archeologists, and ranchers had preceded me on their varied missions. An open skiff at Moab and ten days' provisions, with enough muscular reserve for the upstream pull on the way back, are the only requisites for the journey. Actually, ancient trails and stone dwellings indicate that human beings inhabited this region long before the first Caucasian ventured to the site. No doubt the rainfall was greater in the days when the cliff dwellers lived here.

Without exception the major Colorado River expeditions had come down the Green River rather than the Upper Colorado. This practice, beginning with Major Powell, came about because of better railroad facilities on the Green River. Powell started from the Union Pacific crossing that had just been completed in Wyoming. Many later parties started from the Denver and Rio Grande crossing at Green River, Utah, 117 miles upstream from the confluence.

The still waters of the Green and the Colorado between Moab and the town of Green River aroused great hopes at one time for navigation of the canyons. Several attempts were made to establish steamboat service between the two places, but the hazards of sandbars and riffles were too great. A fifty-five-foot sternwheeler, the *Undine*, plied the canyons for a few trips but was lost in a riffle. The *Major Powell* made a couple of trips but was found to have too deep a draft. One vessel, optimistically called *City of Moab*, was dismantled after an unsuccessful trial and shipped away piecemeal to the Great Salt Lake.

Some years ago, the citizens of Moab persuaded the U.S. Army engineers to survey the canyons in order to remove navigational hazards. The survey showed that twelve riffles of the Green River would have to be dredged and the Slide cleared to make a channel for moderately large vessels. The latter job alone was priced at $100,000 at the low costs of 1909, and nothing came of the proposals. But today these once-still canyons resound to the reverberations of outboard motors; in 1959 more than four hundred boats took part in an annual two-hundred-mile cruise from Green River to Moab.

It is easy to see why the Ute Indians called this region the Land of Standing Rocks. The canyon walls tower on each side to a height of 1,500 feet, rising through layers of stratified rock to the series of pinnacles and minarets that give the region its name. The country is typical of the high plateau that extends through southern Utah and northern Arizona. The

Hal Leich recorded this photograph of Cataract Canyon as "one of the deepest ruts in the world." It was taken about ten miles below the confluence of the Colorado and Green Rivers in Utah.

arid upland, dissected by countless intermittent streams and dry washes, has been eroded into buttes, mesas, and solitary monoliths. The main rivers run in trenches far below the surface of the land and their tributaries, even those that flow only after thundershowers, have carved deep channels into the solid rock as they seek the level of the rivers.

At the mouth of the Green River I followed again in Powell's track—in his wake this time instead of in his footsteps. He had floated down to the confluence twice, in 1869 and 1871, exploring, geologizing, and surveying. The precision of his work under difficult conditions can be gauged by the river elevation that he calculated at the junction in 1871: 3,860 feet above sea level. Later surveys with more accurate instruments placed the elevation only sixteen feet higher.

Powell's fanciful description of the prospect near the confluence hints at the overpowering impression the canyon walls make upon a voyager:

> Away to the west are lines of cliff and ledges of rock—not such ledges as you may have seen where the quarryman splits his blocks, but ledges from which the gods might quarry mountains, that, rolled out on the plain below, would stand a lofty range; and not such cliffs as you may have seen where the swallow builds its nest, but cliffs where the soaring eagle is lost to view ere he reaches the summit.[2]

Strange stuff to find under the prosaic imprint of the Government Printing Office!

I continued downstream at sunset and approached the very line of cliffs that Powell had eulogized, although my 20/20 vision spotted no soaring eagles either at the base or near the summit. This rampart seemed to block the river's course to the west, but when the current swept against the wall it made a sharp curve to the south and soon plunged into the first rapid of Cataract Canyon. A large whirlpool swirled in the outer corner of the bend, where tightly packed debris ranged along the bank. A crude plank bridge, washed down many miles from the region of civilization, balanced intact on the top of a large boulder.

Half a mile below the bend, opposite a wall capped by pinnacles, I camped on the left shore just above the first rapid. Its muttering was a welcome relief from the silence of the upper canyons. I could find no mooring for the boat, so I tied the line to a corner of the ground cloth under my blanket. I hoped this arrangement would wake me up in case the boat broke away during the night, for I had no desire to start walking or swim-ming the 70 miles back to Moab or the 130 to Green River.

As the firelight flickered into embers, I realized that my dreams of many months were coming true. The preliminaries were over and I was on the big river at last. Tomorrow the main event started. This was all right with me; like Tennyson's *Ulysses*, I told myself

> my purpose holds
> To sail beyond the sunset, and the baths
> Of all the western stars, until I die.

CHAPTER EIGHT

Shipwrecked in the Desert

Sunday, August 27, dawned with a gray, misty rain filling the void of Cataract Canyon. After a good breakfast I walked down the shore to the first drop in order to look over the channel. This was the first rough water below Moab and the beginning of a concentrated stretch of whitewater. Actually, the first pitch was an innocent, rock-free chute, with high breaking waves but no other hazards. Just above the rapid, two driftwood boughs leaned against a large rock and a new nailhead showed that campers had recently been there. (This was a relic of the Swain-Hatch expedition, which came down the Green and the Colorado Rivers to Lee's Ferry in July and August of 1933.)

Sailing at 7:30, I resolved to pass the worst of the canyon rapids by nightfall. In a moment the boat approached the first drop, sank over its tongue into high crests below, and glided safely into the quiet outrun. Except for the greater weight of the breakers (resulting from the doubled flow of water), the rapid seemed no worse than the heavy riffles below Glenwood Springs. The second drop, a short distance beyond, also offered no difficulty; the *Dirty Devil* made it with only a flicker of spray on the deck. I was gratified to notice how the new eight-foot oars increased my control of the boat.

But as the morning lengthened the rapids increased in power. The channel became clogged by irregular dams of boulders, some strewn across the riverbed from tremendous rockslides off the canyon walls and some washed into the main stream by small tributaries in floodtime. Instead of undulating through a neat series of haystacks, the river spewed into a confused jumble of broken water. In some places three or four chutes pierced

The treacherous Cataract Canyon of the Colorado River is one of the most difficult stretches of whitewater in North America.

a dam of boulders and offered easy passage amid waves and whirlpools, while in other spots the entire channel was peppered with jagged, half-concealed rocks.

I could well understand, in venturing into the turmoil of Cataract Canyon, why this section of the Colorado has claimed more lives than any other. It is a gigantic trap for the unwary adventurer or prospector who glides down the smooth waters from Moab or Green River in an open boat. Not knowing of the rapids ahead, he might risk his outfit in the first easy drops, hoping for quieter water below. Downstream he would be able to run many more rapids, or carry or line his boat around the bad ones. But finally, especially at high water, he would come to a rapid too turbulent to run safely and with too narrow a shore for lining. Faced with the choice of retracing his way and carrying his outfit around all the rapids he had already run, he might decide to risk the rough water. No doubt some of these decisions led to disaster when the voyager was drowned in the rapids or lost in the arid upland if he scaled the 1,500-foot canyon walls.

The power of the Colorado River is on display in this photograph taken in Cataract Canyon.

But at least one unsuspecting navigator was able to run and line his boat all the way down to still water. When the Kolb brothers made their notable photographic trip in 1911, they met a trapper, One-Eyed Charlie (Smith), laboriously working his way around the rapids in an open skiff, unaware of the dangers ahead. He later wrote them that he succeeded in getting all the way through to Glen Canyon.

Some wild statements have been made about the number of lives lost in the canyon—for example, that fewer men have successfully passed through than have been killed in the attempt. In 1914, the Kolb brothers wrote in *National Geographic* that in the forty-five bad rapids of Cataract Canyon there must have been that many men who had attempted the passage and were never heard from again.[1] The exact roster of casualties will never be known, since there is no way of counting those who entered and those who emerged alive at the lower end. Evidence based on wreckage, human remains, and records does indicate a substantial total.

Late in the morning, as the sun cleared the last shreds of mist from the gorge, I ran a rapid that represented swift water at its best. The canyon walls retreated somewhat from the shore and the river swung around a delta of boulders in two long curves, describing a graceful S-shaped design. The current concentrated in a narrow, rock-free channel that ran along a low cliff on the right and then curved across the riverbed to the other bank. Down the channel for a hundred yards the apex of the yellow current, running at furious speed, tossed in a series of high, steep, and hollow waves, spaced fairly close together. I had a vivid sensation of speed by watching the rocks race past a foot or two from the boat when she approached the cliff. Her motion in the waves was violent. Since the distance from crest to crest nearly equaled her length, she pitched from stem to stern like a rocking chair but took little water aboard. The oars, biting into slower water on each side of the swift channel, tried to wrench themselves from my grip as I rowed against the current to keep her end-on to the combers. Controlling the vessel in her fight with the waters brought a sense of exhilaration that was compounded with speed, excitement, and the satisfaction of riding safely on the back of a tossing giant. It was for this that I had given up my job back east.

All morning I ran merrily through the rapids of the upper canyon, taking the waves as they came and not bothering to land in the excitement of threading a precarious way down the rock-choked river. I ran in hours

Leich titled this photograph of fast water in Cataract Canyon as "Mind your P's and Q's."

what the large parties before me had taken days of lining and portaging to accomplish. Standing in the cockpit facing forwards, with the heavy spray cover stretched tautly across the opening, I had a clear view ahead and guided the boat by pulling upstream, veering across the channel as necessary. The morning, however, was not without potential disaster; several times the boat bumped heavily against submerged rocks and it was soon apparent that she was leaking more than usual. In one rapid the *Dirty Devil* nosed under a huge breaker and buried herself from stem to stern while the yellow foam tossed over my head. Water flooded through the space between the spray cover and my body, filling the cockpit to a depth of half a foot. After bailing her out, I continued the roller coaster ride, unmindful of the warning.

My pride in my whitewater skill, excessive since Westwater Canyon, was shattered just after noon in a more difficult section of the river, which had a drop of twenty-five feet per mile. Seeing a steep pitch ahead where the river humped up in midstream between two boulders and disappeared, I decided to run it without landing to look it over. As I rode over the bulge of water, rowing against the current to slacken speed and maintain steerage way, I saw that she was going over a fall caused by a ledge that extended all the way across the river. In higher water the ledge would have formed a heavy rapid, but at the low stage of late summer it caused a vertical fall that seemed four or five feet high. The water plunged into a deep pool before rampaging downstream into the outrun waves.

The *Dirty Devil* dropped into the pool with a lurch that nearly threw me out. Then I was amazed to see that she was actually traveling upstream, and in a moment the stern sank violently. A backward-rolling wave had carried her under the fall, where the descending flood of water buried her stern. Then she was sucked further back into the fall until her aft deck was pushed under by the torrent's force and her bow reared into empty air. Since I was obviously doing no good with the oars, I jumped onto the forward deck to get the boat back onto an even keel and to keep out of the fall myself. But a sudden upward thrust of the deck threw me overboard. I came to the surface as I was floating past the bow. Luckily at that moment the boat settled for an instant and I grabbed the iron handhold on the bow before it rose again.

For several minutes the boat hung below the fall while I clung to the handle, wondering what to do next. Then, as I struggled to climb back aboard, she somehow freed herself from the pocket of foam between the wave and the fall and began careening down the rapid. In view of the rocks in the riverbed, I had an uncomfortable moment hanging onto the bow of the four-hundred-pound runaway with my legs drawn underneath her. When I somehow scrambled back onboard, she was tossing out of control in the haystacks. Frantically groping inside the cockpit for an extra oar, I located one at last and brought the boat safely ashore at the foot of the rapid, where the missing oar drifted in a whirlpool.

When I looked back at the place, I could see my folly in running the fall without an inspection. Had I seen the wave rolling back into the fall, I would have rowed with enough forward speed to sail through the trap with ease.

After bailing out the scow I had to reload her cargo, which had shifted sternward under the fall. I glanced at my waterlogged watch, a present from my father on my sixteenth birthday, and saw that it had stopped at 12:30 sharp. A stained and water-soaked twenty-dollar bill threatened to disintegrate in my wallet so I put it in the duffel bag. The thought of food had a momentary appeal, but I decided to forego lunch in the hope of running the worst rapids by nightfall.

A glance at the profile maps showed a series of almost continuous cataracts ahead, the river dropping 155 feet in seven miles and in the worst mile 35 feet. The sections of the topographic map had letters at each end to match up with the letters of the next section. The stretch ahead of me, from 204 miles above Lee's Ferry to 197.5 miles above Lee's Ferry, showed p'----p' at one end and q'----q' at the other. I had decided the first time I had seen the maps that it would be a good idea to mind my p's and q's.

This central section of the gorge, above the mouth of Gypsum Canyon, troubled the early expeditions with the severity of its cataracts. Often a party would spend a whole day in painfully lining or carrying their outfit a mile or two along shore. On his first trip Powell described the worst descent in Cataract Canyon:

> We examine the rapids below. Large rocks have fallen from the walls—great, angular blocks, which have rolled down the talus, and are strewn along the channel. We are compelled to make three portages in succession, the distance being less than three-fourths of a mile, with a fall of seventy-five feet. Among these rocks, in chutes, whirlpools, and great waves, with rushing breakers and foam, the water finds its way, still tumbling down. We stop for the night, only three-fourths of a mile below the last camp.[2]

His estimated drop in this case was badly exaggerated, but one that is understandable to any voyager who peers ahead down the foaming, roaring descent. Dellenbaugh, in recording the second Powell voyage (in 1871), made it clear that the party carried or lined their boats around most of the drops in Cataract Canyon. In addition to a desire to safeguard scientific instruments and food supplies in the remote wilderness, a compelling reason for such caution was their lack of proper whitewater technique. Each long, heavily laden boat was rowed forward in the current for steerage way, and the man in the stern with a long steering oar was virtually helpless to maneuver his craft among narrow chutes and boulder traps.

The rapids came in an ever-deepening crescendo. Cowboys say that when the wind is right the roar issuing from the depths of the canyon can be heard several miles away on the plateau, 1,600 feet above the river. James Russell Lowell once wrote that "Milton is the only man who has got much poetry out of a cataract—and that was a cataract in his eye."[3] After

Another view of Cataract Canyon, taken by Leich as he approached his unintended final rapid and the wreck of the *Dirty Devil*.

hearing the roar down the river, I agreed that any attempt to imprison the fury of those waters in verse would be lamentable.

Filled with a proper spirit of humility, I now made it a rule to land at the beginning of a rapid and look over the water ahead. The worst cataracts were formed by large, irregular blocks of sandstone or limestone that had toppled off the canyon's sides, obstructing the current and making it gush through the openings in boiling flumes. Pumps of water rose over submerged rocks and settled on their downstream sides into actual holes in the river—deep depressions not quite filled by the eddying backwash. From the shore I would try to map out the safest route, watching the set of the current among the rocks and picking out landmarks—or often watermarks—to guide me. Sometimes a light ripple on the tongue of a rapid would be a useful guide; sometimes I could steer for a boulder at the head of a drop and then veer sharply to get in the best position. In long rapids I made myself memorize a formula of sailing directions, such as "steer for the right slope of the entrance wave, watch the left-hand hole halfway through, and then pull hard to the left to miss the big rock."

In midafternoon the *Dirty Devil* came to a cataract where rock fragments as big as small houses blocked the river's course. Fifteen minutes of watching the current convinced me that I could make it if I steered with hairline accuracy. A dam of boulders choked the left-hand side and where the dam came to an end, to the right of the river's center, the largest rock rose out of the surging current. At the right of this a narrow flume penetrated the barricade and spilled itself onto the upstream face of a smaller rock. A boiling reflex wave surged back and then the water dropped over a fall to the left of the rock and flowed into a heavy riffle.

Steering carefully down the flume, I avoided the large rock to the left and a sharp pinnacle on my right. I rowed with all my strength against the current to cushion the shock when the punt hit the rock at the bottom of the flume. She surged through the reflex wave and glanced off the rock face, quivering from stem to stern. As she bounced back from the rock she was sucked around a narrow opening and drawn over the fall, plunging downstream into a heaving mass of water where dozens of torrents that had percolated through the barricade finally converged. Rearing and tossing, she rode the lower crests like a charger prancing through the broken ranks of the enemy.

About 4:00 I reached the head of the worst pitch, 203 miles above Lee's Ferry, where the river dropped 35 feet in the following mile. At each drop I would walk ahead to set a course and return to bail out the boat and lash down the spray cover. Several times I saw recent footprints in the sand, indicating that the party that had camped at the head of the canyon had also come down by boat.

The boulder-strewn channel made me wonder whether the rapids would be easier or harder to navigate at high water. During a flood the waves are higher, the holes more dangerous, the current far swifter, and the whirlpools more powerful. At a low stage, on the other hand, more rocks are exposed or are just under the surface and some of the ledges cause waterfalls instead of rapids. A large party planning to carry its boats around the bad places might prefer a low stage. With my four-hundred-pound battleship this was no advantage—I might as well have tried to pack a piano up Longs Peak as carry the *Dirty Devil* along shore.

Several times I wished I had three or four stevedores along so we could hoist the punt on our shoulders and carry her around the worst places. But since there was nothing to be gained by moping around on shore, I would look over the rapids, climb aboard again—not without some reluctance— and let the boat drift ahead to test her seaworthiness in the turmoil. One after another the cataracts dropped away down the canyon. The river surface looked like a series of terraces, the water flowing quietly for a hundred yards or so and then falling furiously through rocky barriers to the next lower level.

Late in the afternoon I reached the worst drop in the worst mile, a wide cataract of churning waves. All across the stream, except for one narrow chute to the left, the river boiled among half-hidden boulders and sharp fragments of limestone. The chute itself, containing a fourth of the river's flow, offered a dubious passage among submerged rocks and larger boulders sprinkled down the channel. At least the steep descent would decide the issue quickly. Fortunately, a light streak of foam played along the entrance tongue, for the drop was so sharp that I could not see over the edge from the boat. Steering for the foam-flecked wave, I maneuvered into position and let her slide over the edge, hoping to miss a bad hole on the right and a sunken rock on the left. Her speed suddenly seemed terrifying. I glimpsed the gulping hole under the starboard oar, saw a black rock fly past on the left, and realized that she was below the drop, splashing and rolling through high, lumpy waves.

It was the climax of the cataracts. Swift water still tumbled down rock-filled river slopes, but it became increasingly easy to find clear passages. Beyond the next mile the canyon turned to the west for a short jog and then resumed its southerly course down an impressive rocky aisle some three miles long. Elated at the ease with which I had overcome the worst that Cataract Canyon had to offer in the thirteen difficult miles since morning, I began to watch the narrow shores for a place wide enough to hold my camp.

The sun had already disappeared behind the western wall of the majestic aisle ahead, though its yellow light still threw into bold relief every pinnacle on the opposite cliff. The brink of another cataract, 199 miles above Lee's Ferry, dropped from sight. Below there, I told myself, I would make my camp. The maps indicated that this was one of the sharpest drops in the canyon, but I determined to end the day with a flourish and run the cataract as it came.

Ten yards above the lip, while I rowed against the current for steerage way, straining to catch a glimpse of the rapids, the bow crunched onto a submerged obstruction with a shock that nearly threw me off my feet. Annoyed at this interference with my piloting, I took off the spray cover and reached below decks for a stout pole to shove her off. Then I noticed that her stern had already begun to swing around to the right, and I knew from experience that she would free herself when she swung around below the rock. But just as the boat reached the point where she was broadside to the current, her stern grounded on a second submerged rock and there she hung, suspended between them. The strong flow of water, running smoothly at perhaps six or seven miles an hour, pinned her against the two sunken rocks like a giant hand from the depths.

Realizing at last the seriousness of the boat's position, I jumped onto the right-hand rock and stood ankle deep in the rushing water. I found a good purchase for the pole and began to pry against the stern. The effect was indiscernible. Then I ran across the decks to the left-hand rock and pried with all my strength. I might as well have tried to move the Washington Monument from its base. The glassy surface of the water did not show a ripple, but the current's force against the flat, upstream side of the *Dirty Devil* must have been tremendous.

Running across the boat to the right-hand rock again, I picked up one of the Moab oars and tried again to pry the stern over the obstruction. First

I used the pole until it snapped off in my hands. Then, hoping the longer oar would give me greater leverage, I leaned on it with my entire weight and broke it off clean. Equally futile were my frantic efforts to lift the boat by the forged handle near the stern. A team of horses on shore and several lengths of logging chain might have done some good, but even then the boat would probably have pulled to pieces before escaping from the river's grip. The two watertight compartments that I had failed to build would not have saved her.

Back in the cockpit for more oars to break, I found that the *Dirty Devil* was already half full of water and settling fast. The current's force had opened a seam where the downstream side pressed against the rocks. Even as I reached below decks for spare oars the scow began to tilt upstream, and the instant her deck coaming came down to the water's level the current rushed in with tremendous violence and accelerated the tilting motion. I clawed my way up the canted deck and jumped onto the right-hand rock, having no desire to be caught beneath her. But there was no great need for haste. Slowly, ponderously, the *Dirty Devil* turned on her beam-ends until her decks were vertical and the current was gutting her out. Still caught on the upstream side of the two rocks, she lay on her side half-submerged, the full force of the current roaring into her cockpit and sucking past her bow and stern.

Now she was lost beyond all hope and as much a part of the river as the driftwood trapped in crevices. My efforts turned from the salvage of the vessel to the salvage of those parts of her cargo that would help me get out of the canyon. This meant food above everything else. As the boat inched into the depths I groped inside her cockpit, holding onto the upper coaming with my right hand and reaching inside with my left. To extend my reach, I let myself down until my legs were drawn underneath the boat, between the two rocks. The pull of the current required a two-handed grip on the cockpit coaming before I could draw my legs up again. I found the best way to reach inside the boat was to hold my breath and duck below decks.

But the river beat me in the race for food, for its swirling waters, scouring the inside of the boat, had carried away everything movable. I cut the lashings that held the duffel bag and the rubber sack below decks, but before I could grab it the duffel bag whirled out of the boat and sank downstream. It held a large part of my food supply as well as the twenty-dollar bill. The mason jars of food had long since smashed on the canyon bottom.

Even the few oranges and onions that floated on the boiling current eluded my grasp. I did not save a single scrap of food from the wreck.

I did salvage the packsack, but this contained little to help me. Perched on the side of the sinking boat, I hastily pawed through it and tossed away the first thing I found—a hand axe. A pair of hobnailed boots, useful for climbing out of the canyon but too heavy to wear through the cataract, followed the axe into the water. I stuffed a pair of woolen socks into my pocket. The other items were of little value so I let the packsack slide overboard and sink, leaving only the rubber sack.

The boat now settled until only a triangular patch of her battleship-gray stern showed above water. The last thing I saw was the gaping lower seam where the rock had crushed her side. Perhaps twenty-five minutes after striking, the scow had disappeared, leaving her skipper half-awash on a sunken rock at the head of a major cataract. I should have known that a thirteen-footer called the *Dirty Devil* was not to be trusted.

Already soaked, shivering, and nearly exhausted, I decided to head for shore before becoming any weaker. Without a boat the prospect down the cataract was terrifying. Ten yards below the rock to which I clung the river narrowed and dropped out of sight, reappearing quickly in a state of turbulence. Some large boulders rose near the right shore just above the drop; between them and my sunken rock, half the river's flow swept downstream over the brink. I nurtured the wild hope of swimming across to the rocks before being drawn over the edge into the cataract. I tightened my life preserver straps and trapped some air in the rubber sack for additional support.

Clinging to the rubber sack with one hand, I pushed away and fought to cross the current. I swam with all my strength for the point of rocks, but the current swept me down and I missed the nearest boulder by a margin of several yards.

The swift water quickly drew me into the turmoil. First came a direct fall over a sunken ledge where the river plunged downward several feet. Exhausted, I gave up hope when I rode over the bulge and dropped into the pool. Down and down I seemed to go, forever. Then, just as I thought I couldn't hold my breath any longer, the life jacket brought me to the surface and I gulped some air before being whirled into the haystacks. Somewhere I lost the rubber sack, so I could use both hands to surmount the combers. The first one broke in my face and submerged me again, but I rode over the next three or four successfully. When the current slackened I drifted into an eddy along the right bank, where the rubber sack floated in a whirlpool. Slowly I swam toward it and drew it ashore at sunset, perhaps a quarter below the wreck. I could hardly stagger on landing.

Upon opening the sack I found that the matches were dry. I lit a drift-wood fire, dried out my clothes, and finally stopped shivering. A quick inventory showed that I had plenty of matches, a pocketknife, a compass, maps of the country, the seven-shot revolver, and fifty rounds of ammunition. My clothes consisted of cotton khaki trousers, a leather belt, a woolen khaki shirt, the kapok life jacket, the two wool socks I had found in the wreck, and one light sandal, the other having disappeared in the rapids. My old felt hat was also claimed by the river.

The rubber sack also held my diary and photographic equipment—two cameras and some film. Knowing that the few necessities would be enough of a burden, I discarded one of the cameras, some writing paper, maps of the lower river, and all the film except one roll taken in the canyon earlier that day.

Finally, I needed to decide what to do and where to go. I was already hungry from having skipped lunch in the excitement of running the rapids. It seemed like a long time since my 7:00 breakfast. I knew I had better get started in the right direction without wasting time. I remembered Stone's comment on finding a wrecked boat and the footprints of two men and a boy in Cataract Canyon in 1909, the year I was born:

> To lose one's boat in such a place is practically to lose one's life, because even if it were possible to climb out, the country being a grassless, treeless, waterless waste, deeply scarred by side canyons that are generally impass-able for a long distance back from the river, a stranger on foot and with-out maps or provisions, especially water, could not possibly reach either Monticello, Moab, or Dandy Crossing, the only places where help might be found.[4]

I realized that my only chance was to prove Stone wrong. At least I had the maps, and one more thing was strongly in my favor. At the age of twenty-four, hardened by many weeks of climbing, swimming, paddling, and rowing, I was undoubtedly at my lifetime peak of physical fitness.

I had four choices of routes: upstream northeast to Moab, downstream southwest to Dandy Crossing at the little settlement of Hite, overland northwest to Hanksville on the Dirty Devil River, or overland southeast to Monticello or Blanding. As the crow flies, Moab, Monticello, Blanding, and Hanksville were all forty miles from the wreck. Since I was no crow, Moab would be about eighty miles up the Colorado canyons, the only route I could be sure to follow. Although I might pick a way alongshore to the junction with the Green River, I knew there were places below Moab where the canyon walls rose vertically from the water, with the whole river flowing down against me.

Between Cataract Canyon and the settlements of Monticello and Blanding towered the Abajo Mountains, a rugged, arid wilderness. Northwest to the Dirty Devil River lay one of the most forbidding regions of the West, the "Robbers Roost" country of broken mesas and vertical canyons, with waterless plateaus stretching away between deep trenches. I had heard too many tales of men lost in that sterile maze to consider the overland route seriously. As the Kolb brothers had written:

> We know one man who did climb out after losing his boat, and who existed for weeks on cactus and herbs until he was finally discovered. He is an able-bodied man today, but has practically lost his reason.[5]

My map showed that it was thirty-six river miles downstream to the Hite post office at Dandy Crossing, a few miles below the mouth of the Dirty Devil River. I was not sure that this small settlement was still inhabited; I knew it was no longer listed as a post office, and Clyde Eddy, after his 1927 voyage, had reported the buildings abandoned. At least I would have plenty of Colorado River water to drink, and if Hite were deserted I still might trace a way north to Hanksville by way of Trachyte Creek or the North Wash. I decided to head downstream.

At my landing place the canyon's walls rose to a great height on each side of the river, mounting by laminated steps from narrow rocky shores that were formed from the debris of rockslides. I placed both of the woolen socks on my bare right foot and tied them to the trouser leg with rawhide to keep them from slipping off. Then in the remaining half hour of daylight I started walking downstream along the right shore, picking my way among sharp rocks and slimy mudbanks. Soon I noticed two white objects gleaming at the water's edge in the twilight. They were onions that had floated out of the wreck. Farther down I found my raincoat, tightly wrapped in its cover, floating in an eddy near shore. These discoveries cheered me greatly—all was not completely lost. About a mile below my landing place I found a good campsite and decided to bed down for the night.

When I had collected a large supply of dry driftwood and started a fire, I roasted the two onions on a spit and ate them for supper. Then I dug into a dry, sandy bank along a wall of boulders. On the unprotected side I built up a windbreak of driftwood logs until I had a narrow trench for a bed. Wearing the life jacket over my clothes, I swathed myself in the raincoat and buried my feet in a heap of sand to keep them warm. For a pillow I used the stout canvas sack my mother had sewn for my diary. With a roaring fire at my feet and a pile of driftwood on hand to keep it going, I settled down to be as comfortable as possible.

The air chilled quickly after nightfall. The evening was clear and the quarter moon, hidden by the canyon wall behind me, illuminated the opposite cliffs in a filmy light, picking out in filigree the towers and battlements of the rugged heights. The irony of my situation dawned on me: I had quit my job in the business world to get out of the rut in which I felt myself sinking, and then had lost myself in one of the deepest ruts in the world. A lesser irony crowded in as well: to have run the worst rapids the upper canyon could show, without a foot of lining or portaging—the first time of record anyone had done so—and then to lose my boat in smooth water.

This quick change in circumstances brought to mind other changes I had experienced—like catching a ride on the Southwestern Limited's tender one spring and lunching with railroad executives at the Transportation Club the next, or sailing into New York harbor one week as a passenger on a trans-Atlantic liner and shipping out the next as a deck boy on the *Sea Thrush*. But these contrasts paled beside my latest change of fortune: one hour the skipper of a well-found craft riding the stream of high adventure, with a month's supply of provisions below decks, and the next a destitute, shivering castaway trapped in a ditch 1,500 feet deep, separated by many miles of canyon and desert from the nearest habitation. This was truly a judgment on my arrogance; I was learning a bitter lesson in humility.

And so ended the lighthearted adventures of the Rover Boy, "With Gun and Camera through the Western Wonderland," and began a grimmer tale, a paradox entitled "Shipwrecked in the Desert."

CHAPTER NINE

Afoot and Afloat

I WOKE UP AT DAWN ON MONDAY—cold, stiff, and hungry. Automatically I looked down at the shore to see how the *Dirty Devil* had weathered the night, realizing with a shock that I would have to furnish my own transportation out of the canyon. I did not waste any time in getting started. Packing the few remaining articles in the rubber sack, I tied it to the top of the kapok life vest so it swung behind my shoulders like a packsack in order to keep my hands free for scrambling up the canyon walls when necessary.

I started walking down the right bank and in a few moments saw the water jug wedged between two boulders. Near at hand floated the remaining oar of the pair I had whittled in Moab. A use occurred to me for this mournful flotsam, so I wrote a short note, placed it in the jug, built a rock cairn around it, and left the oar sticking from the cairn as a signal. I kept the aluminum cap of the jug as a utensil, the only dish of any sort that I had.

Within the next mile I found the boat's seat stranded on a rock and a broken grating bobbing next to a splintered oar handle. More important, in the sand were two sound cantaloupes, miraculously preserved from the sharp teeth of the rapids, as well as four small onions, four oranges, and several lumps of butter mixed with mud and sand. My fortunes were rising again and my hopes rose correspondingly. I put the butter in the aluminum cap, saved the oranges as a water reserve, and decided to ration the onions at the rate of two a day.

Then I kept up a steady pace along the broken shore, jumping along on sharp rock fragments that had fallen from the canyon walls. About a mile below my campsite, I passed the mouth of Gypsum Canyon on the other shore, a winding defile that heads up towards the Abajo Mountains. I briefly reconsidered this as a possible route out of the canyon, but since I did not know the directions to Monticello or the water holes en route, I decided to continue following the river.

Along most of the shore a slope of broken rock lay at a steep angle. This talus slope offered poor footing at best, for the rocks were heaped up at their angle of rest and would frequently slide away under my added weight, bringing fragments higher on the slope crashing down beside me.

Below Gypsum Canyon the river swung west and then northwest in a wide curve, ending the long north-and-south reach where the *Dirty Devil* had been wrecked. The sun followed my slow progress around the bend, beating down more intensely every minute. The evaporation in the dry air was so high and my exertion so great that I stopped to drink river water two or three times an hour. Aboard the *Dirty Devil* I had consumed one gallon a day—no doubt my rate of consumption was now increased considerably. Under such conditions a person deprived of water would truly have a hard time continuing. To protect my head from the sun I folded a Forest Service map of the La Sal National Forest into a peaked paper hat and marched down the riverbank like a toy soldier.

Around midmorning I reached the first place that offered any problems. The talus ended and a sheer cliff of unbroken rock rose from the river. By climbing up the slope, however, I found a narrow ledge forty feet above the water and followed it several hundred yards to the next stretch of rocky shore. A little later I came to a similar cliff, except that its smooth face offered no chance of passage; it was apparent that my only solution was the river.

At this point the big rubber sack again proved its worth, for I took off all my clothes and stuffed them inside, thus using the sack for its intended purpose, since *gummikleiderbeutel* means "rubber clothing sack." The sack looked like an overgrown coin purse; a hinged metal clasp closed tightly on two surfaces of sponge rubber that formed an airtight seal. By allowing the sides to separate and quickly snapping the clasp shut, I was able to trap enough air inside to keep the sack afloat despite its heavy load.

I gingerly let myself down into the water between sharp pinnacles of rock and slimy mudbanks. The sack floated freely behind my shoulders and the life jacket provided enough buoyancy that I could paddle along and enjoy the scenery. The current carried me rapidly past the sheer-walled bank for hundreds of yards until I found a narrow, rocky beach on the right bank where I could land. Chilled by the cold water, I was glad to dry off in the wind and put on my clothes again.

Thereafter I often repeated this performance, sometimes swimming for only a few yards and sometimes for quite a distance. After ten or fifteen minutes my teeth would begin to chatter and my leg muscles would cramp. Finally I became so averse to swimming that I took foolish chances on the cliffs to avoid the chilling water.

But the water was welcome compared to the sucking mudbanks that sometimes stretched between the river and the cliffs. Their sun-cracked surfaces looked solid enough when I ventured out on them, but many times when I was between two points of safety I broke through the dried crust, floundering knee-deep in a slimy green muck and settling fast. Then I would throw myself forward onto my chest, extricate my legs, and slowly wriggle ahead to the nearest solid ground.

A little before noon I reached the mouth of Clearwater Canyon, on my side of the river. A wide delta from this side stream crowded the main river over to the left in a narrow rapid and made a boulevard for the foot traveler. There I found another camp of the party that had preceded me down the river. For an instant I looked ahead, half-hoping to see some boats disappearing around the bend, but a light film of rust on an empty milk can made me realize what a vain hope this was. Kicking the can aside, I headed down the river.

At midday I came to a place where I had to swim to the opposite shore. To avoid a roaring rapid, I swam diagonally upstream until I saw that I would not be sucked over the edge. After I had dressed again I found a cool shadow under the southern wall and opened the sack to see what I could spare for lunch. The two cantaloupes were beginning to spoil—and anyway were too heavy to carry any further—so I ate them down to the rind, thinking with gratitude of Mr. Pariott in Moab and the coincidence that had sent me in his direction five days before.

With my load considerably lightened, I continued along the left bank after a respite in the shadow. Time after time that afternoon I came to sheer cliffs where I would have to perform my strip act, lock my clothes in the sack, and jump into the swirling river, swimming for hundreds of yards beneath vertical or overhanging walls. Between these cold plunges

I plugged steadily along the left shore and watched the miles slowly pass on the topographic map. Late that afternoon, in an aisle where the river flowed south for several miles, I climbed high on the wall and skirted along the edge of a cliff on a narrow sloping terrace that was heavily overgrown with bushes. After a mile of fighting tangled vegetation and edging along ledges high over the river, I came to a floodplain at the mouth of Dark Canyon, a gloomy gorge entering the Colorado from the southeast.

Evening was approaching when I came to the end of the floodplain, where an unbroken wall of rock rose from the water. After looking over the place from a narrow perch on shore, I thought I could never pass it alive. On my side of the river I was faced with an overhanging precipice, impossible to scale or avoid by climbing higher. On the other bank a similar cliff hemmed in the river. And down through the riverbed raged a foaming cataract. The heaving current, running with great speed at the lower end of Dark Canyon, made a sharp bend to the west. Because of this curve, the apex of the current crowded far over to the left, beating against the dank, undercut wall and boiling away downstream in a huge reflex wave that danced with surges and whirlpools amid rock pinnacles. This was apparently the tail end of the rapid where Clyde Eddy had what he called a "narrow squeak" when a boat got away and went careening down the rapid.[1]

Since there was nothing else to do and no point in prolonging the suspense, I undressed and thrust my unprotected body into the current, hoping that no rocks would come into my path. I had an uncomfortable feeling of claustrophobia when the stream seized me and whirled me under the overhanging cliffs. By fending off the cliff with my arms and legs I kept myself from being brushed against the jagged wall. The seething current carried me over the reflex wave, out to midstream through the tail of the cataract, and into quieter water around the next bend.

About a quarter of a mile below the floodplain, the cliff finally broke away and I was grateful to regain the narrow shore on the left bank. Now thoroughly exhausted, I dried off, dressed, and began looking for a place to crawl in for the night. According to the maps I had scrambled and swum seventeen miles since dawn—there was no way to count the miles I had added by my circuitous wanderings. On a narrow ledge thirty feet above the river, I found a bank of dry, soft sand that had drifted in like snow when the river had eddied during the spring freshet. I burrowed a hole into the sand before dark, gathered dry driftwood, and prepared a meager supper. I fried two of the small onions in the aluminum cap with some butter, which was already turning rancid. The resulting dish nearly gagged me, but I forced myself to eat it, down to the last scrap. The best part of the meal was a chaser of muddy river water.

The cool night was clear and the western sky a darkening blue, with the pinnacles and capes of the opposite shore resplendent in the light of the setting moon. I wrapped myself in the rain gear and life jacket and wormed a way into the bank of sand until I was comfortable. I awoke many times during the night to watch the constellations on their march across the sky. I could tell time fairly well by the stars from a summer spent sleeping beneath them. Slowly Scorpio sank in the southwest while the Pleiades and then Orion rose over Dark Canyon in the east. A tremendous cedar stump burned and sputtered until morning. Many times I rolled over in my burrow and looked at it, wondering what the next day would bring. Soon the rippling river was visible again in the reflection from the paling east.

Breakfast on Tuesday consisted of as much Colorado River water as I could swill. Anxious to put more miles behind me before the heat of midday, I started walking as soon as it was light enough to pick my footsteps. All morning I hobbled along the left shore, trying to keep my weight off my right foot, which was rapidly becoming lame. The two woolen socks had already worn through in several places, so I kept turning them over and lashing them around my leg with rawhide.

Mille Crag Bend, named by Powell for the thousand pinnacles on its curving walls, marks the lower end of Cataract Canyon. I had been telling myself since Sunday night that my troubles would be over after passing the last cataracts at the bend, but when I got there at midmorning I found the walls just as steep and the mudbanks just as slimy as they had been above. I slowly completed the 180-degree curve to the north and then the river turned abruptly into a steep aisle five miles long called Narrow Canyon, heading due west. (Actually, there is no break in the walls to distinguish one canyon from the other.) Just inside Narrow Canyon I followed an undercut shelf for a few hundred feet to the next patch of shore. The ledge ended at the head of an overhanging chimney and I had to jump for it, falling about ten feet onto a steep pile of rubble and getting scratched and bruised.

The narrowing canyon walls crowded the talus slope more and more into the river. At noon I had to leave the cool shadow of the southern wall and swim across to the right bank. My strength ebbed rapidly when I began stumbling along the sun-scorched rocks. My jury-rigged headgear blew into the water every few minutes, but I needed the protection and always recovered it. Then a welcome shelter opened itself to me: a huge cleft boulder that offered a shaded seat. I gratefully retreated into its riven entrance and there I rested during the noon hour, too weak to lift my head.

Like a Rock of Ages, this shelter strengthened me to the point where I could again take an interest in life. Feeling that the exigency justified my action, I ate one of the four oranges. This revived me further and several long drafts of river water allayed my thirst.

For the first hour after resting I barely staggered along on the right bank, picking a painful way over heaps of scree below the canyon wall. Then I began to feel better and struck a faster pace, determined to get out of Narrow Canyon by nightfall. Twice I scrambled up the wall through dense scrub growth to avoid banks of mud and quicksand along the river. Fortunately a rim of rock forty feet above the water allowed me to pass safely. When this ended after a quarter of a mile, I had to resort to the mudbanks again. Once I sank through the crust above my knees in a nauseous pool of red and blue muck, seemingly bottomless. When I dragged myself out I almost lost the socks on my right foot, despite the rawhide thongs. The mudbank gulped and sucked noisily after I had extricated myself.

Straight down the aisle of Narrow Canyon rose a sharp peak framed symmetrically between the canyon walls. This was Mt. Hillers, 10,650 feet above sea level at its peak, some twenty miles away in the Henry Mountains, west of the Dirty Devil River. Powell named the peak for his faithful photographer on the second expedition, Jack Hillers, a native of Westphalia who remained with Powell for many years in the Federal Service. His pictures, laboriously made nearly a century ago using the wet plate process, are still among the finest taken on the Colorado.

Halfway through Narrow Canyon I realized I would have to swim the remaining miles to the mouth of the Dirty Devil, since both walls dropped sheer into the river. There being no other choice, I stripped again and prepared for a long swim. The current didn't help me since the water hardly moved. I swam steadily for half an hour in the sluggish current, using the breaststroke, until I had to float and let the life jacket bear my weight. After resting a while, I was able to paddle along for a hundred yards more.

Thus between floating and swimming I came at last to the end of Narrow Canyon. I could hardly drag myself out of the water when I reached a small patch of shore on the left bank, across from the Dirty Devil River. Through a V-shaped gash in the cliffs flowed the stream after which I had so optimistically named my scow. Powell's first party had discovered the mouth sixty-four years before:

> As we go down to this point, we discover the mouth of a stream, which enters from the right. Into this our little boat is turned. One of the men in the boat following, seeing what we have done, shouts to Dunn, asking if it is a trout-stream. Dunn replies, much disgusted, that it is a "dirty devil," and by this name the river is to be known hereafter. The water is exceedingly muddy, and has an unpleasant odor.[2]

Later Powell seemed to regret the unsavory name he had thus chosen and decided to call the stream the Fremont River in honor of "the Pathfinder," who had followed its upper course in 1843. Although fastidious geographers tried to enforce this change of name, the Dirty Devil it is called today—on recent editions of several maps and by the ranchers along its shores—and the Dirty Devil it will be called for a long time to come. The Fremont name, however, still clings to the western branch above Hanksville.

Any thought I might have had about trying to go up the Dirty Devil to Hanksville, sixty or eighty miles by the winding course of the canyon, vanished when I looked at the forbidding walls that hemmed in the river's course as far upstream as I could see. According to the map, the distance was now only two miles to the beginning of a river road at the mouth of the North Wash. This route led five miles further down to Hite, passing a cabin on the way. In any case, I saw there was trouble ahead before I could reach Hite. The northern shore of the Colorado rose in a precipice, and on my side a bold headland gave me some doubts about an easy passage.

I was determined to find a way overland, if any existed, since I had done enough swimming for a while. I fought a path through holly thickets and worked up the face of a sandstone cliff until I found a trail made by mountain sheep, two hundred feet above the river. Three times I almost admitted that the sheep were better mountaineers than I, but in the end I was always able to pass, sometimes nearly slipping off the cliff when the friable rock crumbled under my weight. Then I came to the point of the headland, a sharp cape with a huge standing rock at its extremity, eroded from the massive sandstone. The sheep trail entered an intervening chasm and somehow climbed through it onto a plateau. By scrambling up a holly clump I got a slim foothold on the last ten-foot rise and in a few minutes more I was on the plateau.

It was an easy hour's walk along the high sandstone bench and down to a sandy beach opposite the mouth of the North Wash. For the last time I stripped, drew the clammy life vest with its heavy load around me, and pushed away for the other shore. I was shivering violently when I pulled myself out on the northern bank in the late afternoon; my dry flannel shirt from the rubber sack was welcome.

A short walk across a floodplain brought me to the mouth of the North Wash, a deep cleft that cuts through the barrier of the Orange Cliffs and spews the runoff of thunderstorms into the Colorado. On either side the sheer red walls rose for five hundred feet to the sterile upland. On the eastern side of the wash I found a cave-like den beneath an undercut cliff. Human hands had added a rough lean-to shelter, and on the rock wall of the cave someone had traced a plump feminine figure in soot from a candle flame. Below it were the letters "Kate Smith," a sure sign that I was approaching civilization. Future archeologists may conclude that a cultural link existed between the vanished North Wash cave dwellers and the pre-historic Grimaldi race of southern Europe, who carved plump figurines in ivory twenty thousand years ago.

I found signs of recent occupation in the lean-to and dim wagon tracks circled nearby. But I could not determine which way they were heading—up the wash towards Hanksville or down the river towards Hite. Since it was only a mile and a half to the first cabin on the river road, I decided to walk down before nightfall. I picked up the road that was shown on the map, which was actually just a pair of faint ruts high on a red shale terrace under the Orange Cliffs. I followed them as best I could across a broad bench for about a mile, then down through an arroyo to the flood-plain where the cabin was located. My heart sank when I stumbled out of the ravine and saw a deserted log cabin on the riverbank, its broken door swinging in the wind.

By this time the sun was setting. I had come fifteen arduous map-miles down the river canyons since morning, a day's work that included many extra miles of effort. After drawing water from the river with difficulty, since the shoreline was a treacherous bog, I fixed a supper of one onion, boiled this time without butter. The cabin had a wide stone hearth where I cooked my meal. Although I had no appetite and my stomach was growling, I ate the meager slices and drank off the watery broth. After supper I was so tired that I stretched out by the fire and inadvertently fell asleep on the earthen floor without even wrapping up in the raincoat.

CHAPTER TEN

Hell or Hanksville

DESPITE THE HOSPITALITY of the deserted cabin, I was so stiff and cold on Wednesday morning that I could hardly stand. After limbering up with massage and exercise, I began the four-mile walk along the river road to Hite. Gradually the lame muscles felt better and I hit a steady pace, although my right foot was bruised and blistered.

The road followed a line of low cliffs, crowded close to the river. The wagon tracks meandered through dim shade and other signs of man were evident—a campsite, a wire fence, rusty cans. My apprehension grew as I approached Hite. If the place were deserted I did not even know the way out of the country to Hanksville, some forty-five miles north as the crow flies. There were several possible routes, such as the North Wash, Trachyte Creek (which enters the Colorado at Hite), and the lower washes such as Two-Mile Creek and Four-Mile Creek. Since my strength was nearly gone, I could not afford to make a mistake and have to double back if I lost myself in a blind canyon.

I hardly dared look ahead as I walked around the last turn through a grove of willows. And then I was there—standing before two empty log cabins that were falling into ruin. It was evident that they had not been lived in for many years. Over the door of one cabin was a dim penciled sign, "Post Office," still legible from the days when Hite was a center for placer mining along the upper end of Glen Canyon.

My letdown on finding the ranch abandoned was hard to overcome. I ransacked both buildings in the hope of finding someone's cache of food, but all I found was a litter of empty cans and old bottles. These relics made me realize that I was really getting hungry. At a low ebb of energy, my mind refused to solve this puzzle and I decided to spend the middle of the day at Hite and escape the sun's heat. I filled some old mason jars with river water and settled down under the twig and adobe roof of a sagging porch to reflect on my situation. My food supply was nearly gone, I was already weak and lame, it was fifty or sixty miles to Hanksville by whatever winding route I decided on, I did not know which of the two or three routes to take, and the usual water holes were probably dried up by the long drought. In the face of these uncertainties I gave way to an overwhelming lassitude and took a nap in the early afternoon.

I woke up once to see a large yellow snake in the twigs of the roof over my head. As it stretched its neck down a foot or more to look me over, I looked it over too—and visualized a delicate morsel of snake meat for lunch. At least it would be sweeter than the dismembered grasshopper I had roasted experimentally. A few wild shots from my revolver sent the snake back to its hole, puzzled but unscathed. I also wasted half a dozen rounds on a brace of mourning doves in a dead cottonwood. They didn't seem to mind my target practice and finally flew away in boredom. Then I loaded some high-speed, .22 caliber cartridges and took careful aim at a magpie, holding the revolver with both hands. The heavy charge burst the shell around the rim and lodged a fragment in one of my fingertips. It gave me half an hour's diversion to pick the piece out with my pocketknife.

Had I stumbled into Hite thirty or forty years before, my troubles would have been over. This locality had once been a lively mining center for the upper part of Glen Canyon. Its founder, Cass Hite, operated a ferry at what he called Dandy Crossing and also washed gold from placer bars that barely existed because the gold was too finely divided.

According to Utah legend, Hite attempted to keep out other prospectors by passing the word that there was gold in the lower end of Glen Canyon, near Navajo Mountain. Despite this ruse, the resulting gold rush engulfed the Hite area too, and when the disappointed miners found only worthless "flour gold" instead of nuggets, they went after him. Cass Hite hid out for two years before returning to run a ranch several miles below Dandy Crossing. His brother Johnny Hite was the postmaster for many years at the log cabin post office where I was resting.

In addition to the swarms of placer miners and dredge men who came down the canyon seeking their fortunes, another wanderer came along looking for a different kind of gold. He was Cy Warman, "Bard of the

Rockies," a former railroad engineer and reporter who wrote stories about railroading in the West. According to Ellsworth Kolb, Warman was seeking local color in Glen Canyon when he composed a poem to his distant wife, Myrtle Marie, while staying in Johnny Hite's cabin. Later he persuaded a popular singer in Denver to set the words to music and try the song in his repertoire. It swept the nation as "Sweet Marie" in the 1890s.

While stretched out beneath the sagging porch at Hite, oblivious to the human tide that had flooded and ebbed in this rocky valley, I began to observe the world from a new viewpoint—one that showed my actions in a truer perspective. The futility of my wanderings since leaving home struck me and I realized that my efforts had been doomed from the start. The hawks that flew around the cabin so fast the wind whistled through their wings, the two cooing doves, and even the lizards that scampered around my legs seemed to be engaged in activity more fruitful than mine.

As the sun declined in the west my energy slowly returned. A walk around the ranch showed that the plain near the mouth of Trachyte Creek had once been cultivated, for there was evidence of old ditches and furrows. Cairns and claim stakes on the bench above the cabins attested to the former gold prospecting endeavors in the area. I had noticed many claim stakes along the river below Mille Crag Bend, reminders of the indefatigable prospectors whose wanderings throw doubt on those who say they have discovered valleys in the West never before trodden by the foot of a white man. The absence of old tin cans or footprints does not prove that a region has not previously been visited by a prospector, archeologist, or geologist.

The map indicated that the road ended at Trachyte Creek, where it was succeeded by a trail that continued downstream for a few miles. Since the other end of the road stopped abruptly at the North Wash, I was not sure of the usual route north to Hanksville. By carefully inspecting the wagon tracks and hoofprints, I convinced myself that the latest tracks were heading east and therefore the outfit had left the country up the North Wash. I decided to end my day's inactivity and retrace my steps for six miles to the cave at the mouth of the wash, in order to be ready for an early start overland for Hanksville the next day.

Before leaving Hite I cleaned out a mason jar and an old kerosene can, putting them in the rubber sack to use later for carrying water. The remaining camera did not seem to justify its weight; rather than discard it later in the desert, I left it in the old post office, where I hoped someone would find it and put it to good use. With it I left a note saying that I hoped to reach Hanksville via the North Wash.

It seemed like a long walk up the wagon tracks to the cabin where I had slept the night before. I left another note there and continued across the terrace to the foot of the Orange Cliffs. The sun was setting as I slowly walked along the base of the huge wall. The normal reddish tint of the sandstone was enriched and accentuated by the vivid orange rays of sunset. Mesas and buttes fifty miles away to the southeast loomed sharply against the sky, brilliantly colored by the sun. Nearer at hand the broken plateau fell abruptly into a dark confusion of cliff, pinnacle, and gorge that marked the lower end of Cataract Canyon. Only the river moved in that silent land of tortured sterility.

The clear air chilled quickly in the shadow at the bottom of the wash. At the combination cave and lean-to I built a large fire for warmth and boiled half of my last onion for supper, saving the other half for breakfast. I wrapped up in all my clothing and stretched out on a wide plank inside the shelter, the smoothest bed I could find. Glad of the prospect of action the next morning after the futility of the day, I fell asleep almost before it grew dark.

The shelter of the cave allowed me to sleep soundly all night, undisturbed by the ghosts of wanderers—human or sub-human—who had sought refuge there during past centuries. I awakened early on Thursday very stiff and cold, and again had trouble standing up until I massaged my leg muscles.

A vague yearning for breakfast tempted me to try my marksmanship on a flock of magpies in some willows, with the usual luck. After consoling myself with the last bit of onion, which I ate cold, I crossed a wide gravel bar to the Colorado and sat by the river for at least fifteen minutes, drinking as much water as I could hold. I filled the mason jar and kerosene can and improvised a cover and carrying sling for the jar by ripping up a piece of the raincoat.

About an hour after sunrise I headed up the North Wash, with doubt in my mind about finding water along the way or tracing the faint wagon tracks to Hanksville. A last glance at the Colorado, flowing into the upper reaches of Glen Canyon, brought two-fold regret—first because I could no longer ride its current, and second because it represented the only thing drinkable within an unknown number of miles.

The first four miles wound through a labyrinthine gorge in a series of narrow loops and hairpin bends, with vertical sandstone walls rising five hundred to eight hundred feet above the floor. The canyon bottom was of hard-packed sand and gravel, washed by the last flood and since then almost completely dried out. Occasionally there were soft sand patches, still moist, showing that, in some places at least, water lay not far below the surface.

The North Wash, which was named Crescent Creek on the initial U.S. Geological Survey maps, was first explored in 1872 by a party from Powell's second expedition. One of the damaged boats from Cataract Canyon had been left at the mouth of the Dirty Devil River. When the party reached Lee's Ferry for the winter, Powell sent back a group under his chief lieutenant, A. H. Thompson, to traverse the country north of the Colorado, repair the boat, and return to Lee's Ferry by water. The party included Jack Hillers and Frederic S. Dellenbaugh, the first Colorado River historian. They encountered rough going among the steep washes of the northern plateau, crossed the high ridges of the Waterpocket Fold and the Henry Mountains, and descended into Crescent Creek. Following this to its mouth, they made their way to the Dirty Devil River and found that high water in their absence had swept within a few inches of the abandoned boat.

I had a hot and dry morning since I decided not to drink any of my water supply until afternoon. Around noon, however, I was delighted to find a good water hole in the shade of some massive boulders. I drank as much of the clear, cold water as I could hold, finding it more refreshing than the muddy Colorado, and refilled my containers. Greatly encouraged, I kept on steadily, trying to keep in the shadow as much as possible. Every two or three miles I found another water hole, but since I never knew which one would be the last I always stopped for a good drink, like a sailor on the Bowery in New York.

About 1:00 I rested for an hour at a point where the canyon split into two branches. A triangular patch of bottomland, grassy in spots and overgrown with young willows and cottonwoods, extended down the middle between the divergent gorges. The beauty of the clear, deep blue sky, carved red canyon walls, and dusty green grass captivated me. After resting, I decided to pick the branch coming down from the northwest instead of the eastern one. Wagon tracks a few hundred yards beyond confirmed my choice. Many times that afternoon I lost the tracks entirely, where they crossed strips of bedrock or where drifting sand had covered them. Gradually the canyon walls decreased in height as the wash headed back onto the plateau. In the western wall of a wide glade I found a cave like the ones near Moab; crude picture writing adorned its walls and there was evidence of primitive burials.

About 3:00 some fresh cattle tracks showed up in the sand. Farther along were tracks of a horse and dog, heading north. These recent signs of a cattle outfit indicated water holes ahead. The canyon grew more beautiful in its upper course; glens and grassy glades branched off from the main valley under red sandstone walls. Water became more frequent and the floor was carpeted with grass.

Towards evening I came around a bend to the west through a rocky defile. Startled by the clattering of hooves, I looked up to see two men approaching on horseback. They were prospectors going in to the river, their supplies loaded on a burro. They told me that a vanadium mine was located about twelve miles to the northwest and that I should have no trouble finding it with a full moon for illumination. They generously gave me a can of peas from their limited food supply. Our meeting was so brief that I did not even learn their names.

Around the next bend I took a long rest near a water hole. Since I was within easy reach of a haven, I ate two of the remaining oranges and threw away one that had spoiled. I also discarded the kerosene can but kept the mason jar.

I hoped to reach the mine that night and resumed a quick pace, following the prospectors' tracks whenever there was a choice of routes. At sunset I stopped at a water hole in a meadow enclosed by red rock walls. I lit a clump of dead sagebrush, opened the can of peas with my pocketknife, and warmed up the can over the fire. While the full moon rose over the canyon and the orange glow faded in the west, I devoured the peas and drank off the warm juice. I had never tasted anything better. Then I stretched out on the grass and rested. Again, as at Hite, I mused in the silent land and mulled over my basic goals. Was I right in seeking the solitary, wandering life of a would-be Ulysses (junior grade)? Even the grasshoppers mating on the sagebrush mocked the emptiness of my purpose.

I continued up the wash by moonlight and felt strong enough to walk all night if necessary. Fortunately there was no need to do so. In a few more miles, well after dark, I nearly bumped into a cowboy beneath some willows. He looked at me in surprise and then stuck out a huge paw, saying, "My name's George Waldamont."

In a few sentences I told him about the wreck in Cataract Canyon. He took me over to a loaded wagon, where two grizzled prospectors were starting to build a fire. In the moonlight their seamed, deeply tanned faces looked like old mahogany. Billy Hay, the boss of the outfit, welcomed me with a rich Irish brogue and introduced me to his partner, Tobe Barnes of Grand Junction. They were not a cattle outfit as I had thought at first. Tobe and Billy were going in to the Colorado for a winter prospecting trip down Glen Canyon, and George was taking in their supplies with his team. The wagon was piled high with a load of lumber for a boat they intended to build at the mouth of the North Wash.

I relaxed by the fire while old Billy fixed supper—salt pork, canned corn, potatoes, skillet bread, and coffee. The can of peas only served as an appetizer for me. After finishing this hearty meal we sat around the campfire spinning yarns about the river and the canyon country. Billy had made a number of trips between Hite and Lee's Ferry but had never navigated the rough waters of Cataract Canyon. He had found his way down to the river from the rim of Cataract Canyon on such missions as searching for gold, hunting bighorn sheep, or driving cattle when the season was wet enough for them to forage that far south. Billy told many tales about Hite when it was a flourishing ranch and mining settlement. Johnny Hite at one time had irrigated the bench at the mouth of Trachyte Creek, but the flow gradually dried up until the bench reverted back to desert. No one had lived in Hite for eight or ten years.

Billy confirmed the wisdom of my decision not to go up the canyon of the Dirty Devil River. Sheer walls rising above quicksand shores formed an almost insuperable barrier. "Aye, she's a Dir-rty Divvil," was his laconic comment. After hearing his yarns about the few insane survivors from Cataract Canyon who had stumbled across the desert, I tended to agree with Billy when he said, "Young feller, you was sure in God's pocket!"

George and I crawled under a bundle of quilts for the night, beside the wagon and the grazing horses, but I slept little because of the coffee and the sudden change of diet. My stomach seemed surprised that its vacation had ended.

After a good breakfast at daybreak, I helped the men pack their outfit and get underway. Before leaving I gave them the life jacket. Tobe, who could not swim and who had become nervous at my rough-water stories, insisted on giving me two silver dollars in return. Except for this generous payment I did not have a penny; the empty wallet was still in my pocket but the twenty-dollar bill had been lost with the duffel bag.

When everything was loaded, Billy and his crew pushed off to begin a voyage down the Colorado where I had left it. With regret I said goodbye to these generous hosts and cheerful companions.

Friday was another hot, cloudless day. When the lurching wagons and the riders had disappeared down the canyon in a dusty cloud, I turned north and began again the painful business of putting one foot in front of the other.

Billy said that I had walked twenty miles from the river on Thursday and that it was only six more to the vanadium mine. He told me to follow his wagon tracks up the North Wash for a short distance and then west through a side canyon to the mine. I started off in high spirits with the rubber sack slung over one shoulder by a rawhide thong. I still carried the glass jar full of water, although a small amount spilled through the make-shift cover at every step.

It was easy to trace the fresh tracks made by the loaded wagon and the horses. The fog of anxiety I had known for the past five days was dissipated by the sun of Billy's kindly nature. My tranquility was undisturbed when I saw a herd of beef cattle lumbering up the canyon at full speed, several miles beyond our campsite. They had pawed the earth so vigorously that every trace of the wagon tracks was gone.

In a short while I reached what I thought might be the canyon turning off to the mine, but now I was on my own because Billy's tracks were obliterated. I headed up the side gulch westward for a mile or so, finding nothing but cattle tracks from one wall to the other. When the canyon began turning to the south I decided I must be wrong. I doubled back to the fork and turned due north up the principal branch, still on the lookout for a side canyon.

Mile after mile slipped by as the sun climbed higher into a hot, cloud-less sky. The canyon broadened into a wide wash or arroyo, sun-parched and dusty, its floor strewn with white, round boulders as big as basketballs. In some places the dry riverbed, occupied during storms by a stream of torrential power, extended across the valley for a hundred yards. Water disappeared entirely as I climbed towards the plateau and the sheer rock walls broke away into low clay hills, gullied and ribbed by erosion.

At last, near noon, I could not even pretend I was still on the route to the mine—obviously I had missed the side gulch completely. Now I was well up onto the plateau. A dim trail—or two old ruts—meandered up a shallow gully due north to the top of the tableland.

I debated for a few minutes whether to turn back or to continue across the desert another twenty-five miles to Hanksville. I still had a pint of water sloshing in the jar and a can of tomatoes that Billy had given me. I felt strong enough to push on until midnight. Rather than taking a chance on losing my way to the mine again, I decided to continue across the upland to the little settlement on the Dirty Devil River, following a line slightly west of north by the compass.

This decision was not altogether reasonable. A streak of stubbornness asserted itself and I determined to push on to Hell or Hanksville.

In a few more miles I emerged from the shallow head gully of the North Wash and stood on a high desert plateau, with a clear sweep in all directions. I found myself in the midst of a region weird almost beyond description, the true nature of which had remained concealed from me on the long grind up the North Wash. It was a land where erosion had clawed the earth unchecked by vegetation of any kind. Soft clay deposits had been gouged into raw gorges, gullied mounds, and gashed terraces. The landscape nearby resembled the badlands of the Dakotas at their worst. Then, from the rolling tableland where I stood, the ground fell away to the east into the drop-off marking the labyrinthine canyons of the Dirty Devil River. In the west the plateau was slashed by the corroding headwaters of Trachyte Creek into a thousand seracs of clay. Far to the northwest the blue, hazy Henry Mountains, named by Powell for the noted secretary of the Smithsonian Institution, rose in a jagged wall from the terraced plain. Away to the south the land broke off sharply into the "breaks" so characteristic of the Southwest—the lines of cliffs and terraces at the end of a mesa or plateau.

It takes the impressionistic prose of Zane Grey to do justice to the grim wilderness between the Henry Mountains and Cataract Canyon. The following is taken from *Robbers' Roost*, a novel of the Dirty Devil country:

> Nearer, and to the left, there showed a colossal space of rock cleavage, walls and cliffs, vague and dim as the blank walls of dreams, until, closer still, they began to take on reality of color, and substance of curve and point. Mesas of red stood up in the sunlight, unscalable, sentinels of that sepulcher of erosion and decay. Wavy benches and terraces, faintly colored,

speckled with black and gray, ran out into the void, to break at the dark threads of river canyons.

All that lay beyond the breaks of the Dirty Devil.

Here was a dropping away of the green-covered mountain foothills and slopes to the ragged, wild rock and clay world, beginning with scarfs of gray wash and rims of gorges and gateways of blue canyons, and augmenting to a region that showed Nature at her most awful, grim and ghastly, tortuous in line, rending in curve, twisting in upheaval, a naked spider web of the earth, cut and washed into innumerable ridges of monotonous colors, gray, drab, brown, mauve, and intricate passageways of darker colors, mostly purple, mysterious and repelling. For miles not one green speck! Down in there dwelt death for plant, animal, and man.[1]

As I trudged along in the heat of midday, I began to realize how helpless a man on foot becomes when placed in the midst of the desert. On horseback one has a chance of getting somewhere. In relation to the blue sawtooth of the Henry Mountains on my left and a row of buttes twenty miles to my right, I hardly seemed to move from one hour to the next.

At noon I reached a dusty road that ran from the vanadium mine into Hanksville. According to my reckoning I was nearly halfway between our camp of the night before and Hanksville. Soon after reaching the auto road I took my first rest of the day, on an eminence called Lone Cedar Flat, where the only tree in twenty miles cast a small shadow. After dozing for an hour, I woke up refreshed and continued across the wavy desert. Many miles to the southeast I could see a deep notch on the skyline where Cataract Canyon bit into the plateau. It seemed incredible that I had covered the intervening distance on foot. This was my farewell look at the Colorado canyon country.

My route north lay across an undulating upland that was broken from time to time by raw arroyos draining east from the Henry Mountains into the Dirty Devil River. As the road dipped into the gulches I searched them vainly for water. I was becoming thirsty but decided to save what little water I had for as long as possible.

All afternoon I stumbled along in the dust, my glance seldom raised higher than the ground two feet ahead of me. Time after time I mounted a frozen wave of desert and looked ahead, hoping to see the plateau sloping down to Hanksville—instead just seeing more shimmering ridges. The Henry Mountains slowly passed by on my left side until late in the day they lay behind me. On the upper slopes of the ravines I could see timber, which in heated imagination meant cool streams dashing through wooded gorges. Although I hadn't drunk a drop of water since breakfast, I didn't touch the remainder in the mason jar.

At last the hot sun sank behind the mountain peaks in a bath of crimson and the moon rose over a weird line of buttes fifty miles away, near the Land of Standing Rocks. A herd of thirty or forty magnificent wild horses stopped romping over the plain long enough to watch me from several hundred yards away. Suddenly, on signal from their leader, the mustangs wheeled in formation and thundered away in a disappearing cloud of dust.

By evening I was approaching exhaustion. Just before dusk I sank down near the road and opened the can of tomatoes that Billy had given me. The liquid and the moist pulp refreshed me greatly. When I resumed my hobbling walk I noticed a dust cloud coming up from the direction of Hanksville. Half an hour later the truck that was raising the dust reached me. It belonged to the vanadium mine and was taking in a load of provisions. Horace Ekker, the driver, gave me a drink of water from a desert water bag and handed me some sweet, ripe peaches. He told me I was about nine miles from Hanksville.

When the truck had gone I ambled along with renewed energy, resolving to reach town that night. The evening was cool and the road unmistakable in the moonlight. But in my impatience to arrive I forgot how long nine miles of walking can be under the best conditions. Hour after hour seemed to pass with no result. It was the longest nine miles I had ever walked. A dozen times I thought I saw a cluster of houses ahead, only to realize that I was looking at a row of rocks. I was having hallucinations by the time the road finally dropped down a high escarpment into the Dirty Devil River valley. Lights flashed before my eyes and every rocky outcrop was a monster or a demon. At last, a little after 10:00 p.m., I indisputably saw a row of Lombardy poplars near the river. A barn and a haystack loomed out of the shadows. At the edge of the village a man was tending an irrigation ditch and singing "The Utah Trail" in the moonlight. In that setting it seemed altogether appropriate.

I walked up to the other side of the irrigation ditch and in a feeble, croaking voice tried to explain my appearance. I had little success at first. Finally making some sense out of my incoherent discourse, the man showed me the way around the deep ditch and walked with me to the village. His name was Raymond Maxfield and he had just returned from a two-year mission for the LDS Church to Minnesota. It was his first night back in the old homestead with his bride. He took me to his ranch on the other side of the village, where I spent a few minutes trying to drain his cistern dry. I was glad to throw away the mason jar and its unused contents. He gave me a comfortable bed on the porch of a small log cabin, where I sank into a bundle of quilts in thankful exhaustion.

CHAPTER ELEVEN

Farewell to the Colorado

L ATE THE NEXT MORNING, when I finally awoke, I found myself in a
paradise. An irrigation stream bubbled past the cabin where I had
been sleeping and a leafy orchard shaded the grounds. In the distance
green hayfields stretched between rows of Lombardy poplars.

When I tried to get out of bed I found that I had become stiff and sore
in every muscle. A blister the size of a half dollar rose under the thick hide
of my heel, where the tattered socks had worn completely away. My ragged, mud-caked clothing, my bleached hair, unkempt and uncut, and my
unshaven, sunburned cheeks marked me as a desert rat from the canyon
country.

The inhabitants of the substantial log ranch house were also just bestir-
ring themselves. I met my gracious hostess, Mrs. Maxfield, as well as Riter
Ekker, brother of the truck driver from the night before, and Mrs. Ekker.
About 9:30 we sat down to a breakfast that seemed more like a banquet—
cereal and cream, pancakes, eggs and bacon, tomatoes, hot biscuits with
preserves, and milk. After the others had finished they sat fascinated by my
appetite until late in the morning while they told tales about Billy Hay and
the canyon country.

When I asked about getting overland to Green River on the railroad,
Raymond Maxfield advised me to go up to the main road in the village,
where I might have a chance of picking up a ride sixty miles across the
desert. I thanked him for his generous hospitality and hobbled through
the little Mormon settlement to the post office. Since there was no store of
any kind in town, I looked around for someone with whom I could make
a trade. A lanky cowboy ambled towards me from a side street. When I

hailed him, I learned he was Clive Meacham, a sheep and cattle rancher. Squatting on the high heels of his fancy cowboy boots beside a shaded irrigation stream, he listened to my proposition.

I told Clive that I would be willing to trade my revolver for a watermelon, a pair of old shoes, two meals, and a place to sleep that night in case I couldn't get out across the desert. He considered the deal at length, inspected the revolver closely, and then accepted. That was the last time we mentioned the business of bargaining—after that I was his guest.

We walked to his log house and lolled around on the lawn under the poplars. Then Clive brought two ripe watermelons from the garden and went to fetch a pair of old shoes. I tried them on and found they fit perfectly. All through the rest of the day Clive and I sat under the trees eating watermelons and cantaloupes, enjoying the idyllic life of lotus eaters. Now and then neighbors stopped by to spin a few yarns and share the sweet fruits of the garden.

Clive lent a sympathetic ear to the story of my forty-mile walk the day before; his horse had once run away near the rim of Cataract Canyon and he had walked thirty miles back to camp in his high-heeled cowboy boots.

At noontime, we had a full dinner of corn, squash, potatoes, and gravy. Clive, his brother, and I ate our fill and then retired to the lawn. Then the womenfolk and the children had their time at the table. Late in the afternoon I walked to an irrigation ditch behind a clump of trees for a bath. That night we had another meal of fresh vegetables.

Clive and I got along well. He explained that the summer's work of haying had just been finished and that the men around town were enjoying a loaf. Hanksville consisted of about a dozen Mormon families, most of them related. They owned extensive range lands, grazed by cattle and sheep, for a radius of thirty or forty miles from town. One member of a family at a time went out with the stock while the rest did work around town—irrigating, haying, and fruit picking. Almost everyone in the village was wealthy in terms of livestock. Clive pointed out a little girl running around in rags who owned eight hundred head of cattle on Waterhole Mesa.

During a moist season the stock was taken as far south as Cataract Canyon along the plateau. In the drought years of the 1930s, however, the herds stayed close to the Dirty Devil River, which at Hanksville flows through an open valley before entering its tortuous canyon. The country I crossed from Hite, once a good cattle range with abundant grass, had become a desert. Its story is a vivid object lesson in the need for good soil conservation practices. In the 1870s, when Hanksville was settled, the surrounding countryside provided a lush cattle range and the Dirty Devil was a pretty little river flowing between grass banks. The number of cattle increased, and then sheep were introduced and allowed to range without control. They grazed so closely and their sharp hooves cut the sod so badly that the hillsides began to gully during rainstorms. After several decades of this abuse, the Dirty Devil became a raging torrent following each thunderstorm but was reduced to a muddy trickle between rains, lost on its wide, sterile floodplain. The river and its tributaries were eating back voraciously into the clay hills. In the spring of 1933, a flood came off the Henry Mountains through a little ravine in Hanksville and chewed away acres of good irrigated land.

Clive told me that since Hite was abandoned a number of years before, George Waldamont had the only ranch near the Colorado, twenty miles up Trachyte Creek. There he lived alone many miles from the nearest settlement, coming into town only once or twice a year. Clive himself had spent an entire year with his family's flock of sheep in the Henry Mountains, protecting the stock from bears and pumas. At times when the flock was unguarded, bears had slaughtered a dozen ewes in an evening, ripping off their udders for the milk. He also said that sheep can go for thirty days without water if the range is moist and the grass is juicy enough. Once a year the Hanksville ranchers drove their sheep across the desert sixty miles to the railroad at Green River.

The herd of wild horses I saw on the plateau were known to range sixty or seventy miles from the nearest water hole. A short time before, some men had come in with airplanes to round up the horses for dog food, but the herd had broken out of the corral in which they had been trapped.

Clive told me that "Phoenix" Jim Bridger was still alive and working for the Meacham boys with their 2,500 head of sheep in the Henry Mountains. Phoenix Jim was the half-breed son of *the* Jim Bridger, a legendary figure in the history of western exploration—the trapper who brought back tall tales of the wonders of the Yellowstone country and embellished them so vividly that the basis of truth in his statements went unrecognized. Long before the journeys of John C. Fremont, Jim Bridger was trapping beaver in the canyons of the Green River and trading with Indians from the Yellowstone to the Rio Grande.

Clive was as much interested to learn about city life back east as I was to learn about the customs of his remote little ranch town. He had been to Green River several times on the annual sheep drives, and had visited Grand Junction once. The chief thing that impressed him about life in Grand Junction was that shopkeepers washed off their sidewalks every morning with water—that precious fluid so highly prized along the Dirty Devil. Clive liked to read magazine stories about life in New York City, in the same way that a shoe clerk on the East Side devours western stories in pulp magazines.

Before turning in that night, Clive arranged to get me a ride across the desert with Herb Weber, who was driving to Green River the next day. Clive lent me some blankets and I found a comfortable berth in the shadow of a haystack.

After breakfast with the Meachams on Sunday morning, I told them goodbye and thanked them for their bountiful hospitality, which had far exceeded the agreement between Clive and me. On the way to the Webers' house I could not help noticing that several young ladies were just getting up from their beds, which had been moved into the front yards for the summer in accordance with an old Hanksville custom. I had to admire the dexterity they displayed in changing from sleeping garments to dresses in public.

Herb Weber was ready to leave at 10:00. Four of us crowded into his little 1929 Dodge sedan, among heaps of baggage, and were on our way across the Dirty Devil east into the desert, away from the pleasant fields and orchards of Hanksville into a waste of sand, rock, and clay penetrated by two faint ruts. Herb's uncle, whom I had met on the mine truck Friday night, accompanied us. He had come into Hanksville to get signatures for a petition to build a road to Green River. The only existing road came in from the west, thus making the distance to Green River hundreds of miles unless one had the hardihood to take the shortcut we were following. The other passenger was Herb's young son, who was taking his first trip out of Hanksville to go to school in Green River.

We had rough going for the first two hours—into gullies, around knobs, over sharp rises, and through heavy sandbanks. Then we found easier going across an extensive plain south of a curious formation called the San Rafael Swell, a huge sandstone reef rising out of the sand several hundred feet and stretching for a number of miles from east to west. This was the site of a major uranium strike in the 1950s.

Around noon, under the hot desert sun, our crate coughed a few times and stopped. Herb announced that we were out of gas—thirty miles out in the desert. Fortunately, the tank was nearly full and the trouble was centered in the vacuum tank. After siphoning out some gas and running it into the vacuum tank, everything went well for another ten miles until we scraped our pan on a high boulder and began to lose oil at an alarming rate. We plugged the hole with a stick of wood and drained oil from the hydraulic brakes to add to the small amount left in the crankcase. A few miles farther the engine overheated and we had to stop again so Herb could build a fire, melt a can of cup grease, and pour the liquid into the crankcase. We were all glad to turn in at a cattle ranch on the San Rafael River, the only habitation between Hanksville and Green River, where we replenished our oil supply.

The rancher's wife gave us a drink of water and all the watermelons and cantaloupes we could eat, but cattle raising on the desert seemed to be difficult, for the San Rafael River was a bed of dry sand and the cattle had to be watered at a small artesian well.

We finally rolled down the hill into Green River at 4:00 that afternoon, and no further persuasion was required for me to agree with Herb's uncle that a road was badly needed. With the two dollars that Tobe had given me I went to the telegraph office in the railroad station, hoping to send home a request for money. When the agent told me that the local bank had closed the year before and there was no way to send funds into town, I explained my situation and asked his advice. He said the nearest town where I could have money sent was Moab and then Grand Junction, adding that there was a rattler heading east in the morning for Grand Junction and the best thing I could do was grab myself an armful of boxcars. This appealed to me as sound advice.

When I had rented a room for the night, I bought a razor and some soap and after three shaves decided that most of my whiskers had been removed, along with some sunburned skin. My landlady promised to wake me up in time for the morning freight train—most of her guests left town that way.

Sure enough, she called me excitedly the next morning; the eastbound manifest freight was rolling down the hill to the water tank. I barely had time to dress, throw the rubber sack—smelling of rancid butter—over my shoulder, and run to catch the rattler before she pulled out. Climbing onto a flatcar loaded with lumber, I perched on a huge fir beam beside a dozen hoboes and began to accustom myself again to the environment of the road—the noise, wind, soot, vibration, and hearty companionship; the professional tramps, absconding cashiers, reckless speed kids, sodden wastrels, and skylarking college boys—that told me I was back where I had been two years before: on the bum. The class of 1929 hobo was on the road again, this time by necessity rather than choice.

With a mixture of emotions, I watched the Green River flowing placidly beneath the railroad bridge as we highballed out the yards. One hundred and seventeen miles below lay the Colorado River and Cataract Canyon. Every successful Colorado expedition had gone down the Green River past this point; the bridge that we were crossing had been, for most of them, their last glimpse of civilization before entering the canyon country.

The train labored on the upgrade for many miles east of the river. I decided to unload at Thompson, a settlement where the highway branched off for Moab, to call on friends like the Petersons and to see if I could pick up a job with the U.S. Forest Service. The station agent had told me the train would stop there, but she showed no sign of slowing down. I climbed down the iron side-ladder of the flatcar, tossed off the rubber sack, and hit the cinders running forward as fast as I could. But the train was doing twenty-five or thirty miles an hour and I could not keep my footing. I took an eggbeater fall, as a skier would say, in a tangle of flying arms and legs beside the flashing wheels, sprawling on my chest and skidding across to the next track. When I picked myself up I found a few cuts and bruises along my arms, but I was not badly hurt.

The risk I had taken proved to be in vain, for I stood at the highway fork all day long without getting a ride. At noon, a traveling salesman invited me to the hotel for lunch. During the afternoon, I often went into the crossroads store to buy cheese or candy bars for my gnawing hunger, until I had only a few cents left of the money Tobe had given me. The fat store-keeper took a fancy to my rubber sack, visualizing the fun he could have in using it as a grotesque, oversized coin purse. Every once in a while, he would come out and offer me a little more for it. He got up to a dollar but I always refused. It had become a symbol for me—representing, perhaps, the last shred of my former glory as Ulysses (junior grade).

About 5:00 I gave up trying to get to Moab and hailed a ride for Grand Junction. At sunset, we were passing the high sandstone plateau near Westwater Canyon. To the north, on the Book Cliffs, we saw the bright blaze of a brush fire like an evening star. Though I didn't realize it at the time, I had passed the parting of the ways to the future. Back towards Moab was the West—the chance to become a uranium millionaire, perhaps. More likely, I would have built another boat, disappeared into the canyons that fall, and never come out again. The road I was traveling to Grand Junction led east—to white-collar jobs again, a family, and a career in the federal civil service, about as far removed as one can imagine from the lone-wolf life of the Colorado canyons.

For several years afterwards, in the late winter, I would draw plans for a new cataract boat and write up a grub list, but I never made the break again. Gradually I capitulated, became a loyal organization man like my classmates in big business and big government, and joined the Home Guard at last. Today the canyon country seems as dim and shimmering as fifty miles away on the noonday skyline. Like a Maxfield Parrish painting, filled with fair dreams and purple fantasies, the memory of the Colorado River fades away to the far horizon.

AFTERWORD

Jeff Leich and Harry Leich

HAL LEICH AND HIS BOOK: A HISTORY AND A REFLECTION

IN 1933, HAL LEICH SET OUT to accomplish his dream of becoming the first person to single-handedly navigate the Colorado River from its source to the Gulf of California. He based his trip on the Colorado River expeditions of John Wesley Powell in 1869. This book is the chronicle of that adventure.

Biography

Harold Herbert (Hal) Leich was born February 16, 1909, in Evansville, Indiana, the second son of Herbert and Marcella Jacobi Leich, both natives of Evansville. Hal's great-grandfather, Johann Heinrich Leich, had emigrated with his wife and five children from Germany's Westphalia to America after the revolutions of 1848. They came by sailing ship from Hamburg to New Orleans, then by paddle-wheel steamer up the Mississippi and Ohio Rivers to Evansville, where in 1854 the oldest child, Hal's grandfather, founded a wholesale druggist firm titled Charles Leich & Co.

Growing up in a house just one block from the Ohio River in the steamship era had a lasting influence on Hal's life. From an early age he was attracted to rivers and to water travel, manifested in an early interest in sailing ships and the nautical life, later by trips down the Yellowstone and Colorado Rivers, and, much later in retirement, by his time spent as an environmental writer and activist advocating for clean water supplies.

A Leich family friend and Dartmouth College alumnus, Louis Benezet, superintendent of Evansville schools at that time, steered Hal to Dartmouth in Hanover, New Hampshire, which he entered in September 1925 at the age of sixteen. He became active there in the Dartmouth Outing Club (DOC), an organization that introduced students to the outdoor life through hiking, skiing, and other sports. While at Dartmouth, Hal participated in several DOC events, which in retrospect have a degree of historical interest for the White Mountains region. For example, he was a member of a DOC party that in 1926 made a Christmas vacation trip to the summit of Mt. Washington to take meteorological observations. This trip was the inspiration behind the founding of the Mt. Washington Observatory, still extant, by Joe Dodge and Bob Monahan, also members of that 1926 group.

In 1927 Hal participated in the first downhill ski race held in the U.S., a DOC event on Mt. Moosilauke in New Hampshire. He wrote excellent accounts of these events in his diary and letters home. In 1928 he spent a week working in a logging camp in the New Hampshire forest, and again he left in his writings a valuable account of a long-vanished life. He graduated from Dartmouth in June 1929 and spent the summer traveling in Europe and visiting relatives in Germany.

During the Great Depression, Hal held a variety of jobs that appealed to his sense of adventure and gave scope to his wanderlust: deckhand on a coastal freighter, serviceman for Sunbeam Electric and a similar job for Sears, and traveling salesman for Maxwell House coffee. Between these positions he took several extended river trips in homemade boats, including a trip down the Yellowstone in 1930 and an attempt in 1933 to run the Colorado from its source in the Rockies to the Pacific Ocean. Both these river trips are chronicled in this volume.

In 1934 he took a federal civil service exam in San Francisco and landed a job writing examination questions for the Civil Service Commission in Washington, DC. With a break for service during World War II in the U.S. Navy, from which he retired as a lieutenant commander, he spent his entire professional career with the Civil Service Commission. He was awarded a master's degree in public administration from American University in 1955.

He retired as chief of the Policy Division in 1972. During his career he received the Commissioner's Award for Distinguished Service and assisted in the reform of the federal pay system and the organization of the fledgling Environmental Protection Agency. He authored many articles for professional journals in personnel management and public administration.

In 1941 Hal married Cora Louise McIver (1912–1971), the daughter of Brigadier General George Willcox McIver (1858–1947) and Helen Howard Smedberg (1869–1953). We are Hal and Cora's two sons, Harold McIver Leich and Jeffrey Renwick Leich, born in Washington, DC. In 1947 the family moved to suburban Bethesda, Maryland, where we grew up and where Hal lived until his death on September 9, 1981.

In his years in Washington, Hal was active in a number of outdoor organizations and was an early president of the Ski Club of Washington, DC. He was an active member and sometime officer for many years in the American Canoe Association and the Potomac Appalachian Trail Club, and he authored several articles and book chapters on canoeing and whitewater opportunities in the environs of Washington. On one of his skiing treks to West Virginia, he discovered the potential of the Canaan Valley as a ski area and helped to promote that discovery.

After retirement from federal service in 1972, he wrote about water pollution issues and the need for clean water, contributing columns and articles to *BioCycle*, *Small Town*, *Bulletin of the Atomic Scientists*, *Compost Science*, and other publications. An environmentalist ahead of his time, his particular interest and concern was clean water and sanitation. This is evident from the titles of some of the articles he authored, such as "The Terrible Toilet" and "The Sewerless Society." He participated in several important national and international environmental conferences, including the United Nations Conference on the Human Environment (Stockholm, Sweden, June 1972) and the Third National Conference on Individual Onsite Wastewater Systems (Ann Arbor, Michigan, 1976). About four months after being diagnosed with a brain tumor, he died on September 9, 1981. He is buried with our mother, Cora, in Evansville, Indiana.

Writing This Book

Tackling the Colorado single-handed places Hal among the legendary figures who made the voyage. He was inspired by the Powell and Loper expeditions, and he quotes from their experiences throughout his writing, very much aware of their insights from point to point. Although Buzz Holstrom would later achieve public acclaim for his solo navigation from the source of the Colorado River to Lake Mead, Hal was the first to have made the solo trip as far as he did, from the source to Cataract Canyon. He made a photographic record of the Colorado in 1933 as well, capturing images of the river before it was dammed and landscapes were lost.

Hal began writing this book literally during the 1930 and 1933 river trips. Using a practice he followed most of his life, he wrote letters home on lined, hole-punched notebook paper. He also kept detailed notes on the same kind of paper and later integrated these into a binder with his letters—retrieved from recipients—to form a detailed record of his adventures in chronological order.

As his sons we remember, beginning in the 1950s, his evening trips to the basement to work on a book-length account of his adventures. This was inspired by an inquiry from Otis "Dock" Marston, the Colorado River's legendary historian, which led to correspondence and a long friendship. Hal ultimately produced three complete versions, dated 1958, 1969, and 1978, all typed by him on a small manual typewriter. He used various titles and subtitles for the proposed book, including *Castaway on the Colorado*, *Rapids and Riffles*, and *Alone on the Colorado*. Hal made several attempts beginning in the early 1960s to find a publisher for his manuscript, but never succeeded. After his death, his second wife, Marian Nash, tried a number of times to locate a publisher, again without result.

The present edition is essentially the 1969 version, with some minor deletions and editing in the earlier chapters and an addition from the 1978 version of a substantial amount of text specifically about the 1933 Colorado River trip. The 1978 version is about 50 percent longer than the 1969 one, and while it contains much information—particularly in the early chapters—that is quite interesting to us but less relevant to his river adventures in 1930 and 1933.

Location of Sources

We have donated the original manuscripts, diaries, letters, and photographs related to Hal's Colorado River adventures (including all three complete typescript versions), as well as his post-retirement writings on clean water supplies, to the Marriott Library Special Collections Department at the University of Utah, Salt Lake City. They are available for use there; a finding aid to the papers is accessible online: http://db3-sql.staff.library.utah.edu/lucene/Manuscripts/null/Accn1973.xml. Some of the textual materials are also available in the Otis R. Marston Papers at the Huntington Library, San Marino, California (http://www.huntington.org).

REFLECTIONS

By the time we were born in the 1940s, Hal's Colorado River trip was in the past. He had settled down to a career in the federal government and to family life in the Washington suburbs. Nevertheless, he didn't turn his back on his love for nature and adventure. Throughout his life, he maintained his interest in the outdoors, in rivers and water and mountains and snow, in the environment, in adventuring and exploring what was out of sight just around the corner, and in boating, skiing, and hiking. The restlessness of his early twenties gradually diminished as he aged, but adventure and outdoor recreation would always be part of his life. Hal's interest in and commitment to family, excellence, and integrity also grew as he himself grew older.

As his sons, we saw sides of him not evident in the account of his river trips. Hal was a talented writer and poet. He was also an amateur musician (he played violin, harmonica, and concertina), organic gardener, square dancer, creative sketcher, unexcelled handyman around the house, sometime PTA president, talented photographer, and devoted husband and father.

He maintained frequent contact with his parents, siblings, cousins, and other relatives. He was a hero to our Reardon cousins, the children of Hal's sister Ann, who welcomed his visits to their summer camp, bringing stories of his adventures and hobo songs he would sing while playing his concertina. They remember him as a favorite and beloved visitor—tall and handsome, with his warm presence, enthusiasm, and great energies and interests.

At home in Bethesda, he was always actively involved in our education and recreational activities. In fact, the earliest memories we each have in life are of hikes, ski trips, picnics in parks, and canoeing expeditions with him leading the way. He planted seeds that we have nourished in our own lives today as well. We both followed him to Dartmouth for our undergraduate educations. Harry, his older son, based in Washington, DC, has spun his love for adventure into a life that has involved frequent travel to Russia and Eastern Europe. Jeff, the younger son, has, with his own family, lived his life in the mountains of New Hampshire, focused on skiing and the outdoors.

Hal's account, which has never before been published, brings the rich personal perspective and photographs of an adventurer on the Colorado River in the early 1930s, and adds a new chapter to one of our great national experiences. We are happy to introduce Hal and his story to others through this book. It may have happened a long time ago, but it is still fresh.

REACTION OF HAL LEICH'S PARENTS TO HIS RIVER TRIPS

L ETTERS WRITTEN TO HAL LEICH by his parents, Herbert Leich and Marcella Jacobi Leich, have been saved, and provide interesting commentary on his river trips. Hal wrote his parents in Evansville, Indiana, as time permitted during the trips and related his latest adventures, often in some detail and occasionally including photographs as well. Hal's parents had conflicting reactions to their son's wanderings: they liked reading about his latest adventures on the river, but were seriously concerned about his safety and about the fact that, although a college graduate, he'd been unable to find stable employment.

During the 1930 Yellowstone trip, his mother wrote,

> I am glad that your guardian angel is hovering over you for if he weren't, I am afraid you wouldn't be here to tell your wild adventures. Luckily, the waves did not engulf you and you suffered no further harm than getting soaked; still my heart stood still when I read of the danger you were in.[1]

Reflecting the worsening economic depression gripping the country in the early 1930s and expressing a mother's natural concern for the safety of her son (then only twenty-one) as well as for his future, Marcella wrote a few days later,

> Business naturally is very bad and I doubt if we pull through. The inventory is very disappointing and father and the uncles are at their wits' end. Don't you think you had better come home and begin looking around for something stable? It would relieve father's mind if you were settled and had a future before you. I know it doesn't cost us anything for your up-keep, but you aren't getting anywhere with your roaming. . . . Things have changed mightily in a few years and bad weather, crops, business conditions . . . have got us where we are. I am not exaggerating, my dearest boy, I wish I felt that I were, things look very bad—so make up your mind to come home soon.[2]

In August 1933, when Hal was twenty-four and in the early stages of his Colorado River adventure, Marcella wrote,

It has been quite a long time since I wrote you, but I have been waiting for you to reach Moab before sending you a letter. We received your packet and were much entertained reading your diary and seeing your splendid views. You had some thrilling and to judge from your accounts very dangerous experiences and now that you are over the worst part of the rapids, we hope that you will be content to take it easy. I'm glad you made it with nothing worse than a wounded hand which must have been bad enough.[3]

Again in 1933, Hal's mother wrote, having apparently just learned of his shipwreck in Cataract Canyon and the long hike back to civilization,

I can't tell you how sorry I am that you had such a terrible experience but thank God, you survived it and I sincerely hope will not suffer any bad effects later on. I can't understand how you ever had the strength or willpower to struggle on through miles upon miles of hot sand and burning sun. It is most unfortunate and I can well understand how disappointed you must feel. One thing you have gained from the affair is material for thrilling adventure stories, much more exciting than if you had reached your goal without any mishaps. Do give up the idea of trying it again as it isn't worth it. If you were on an expedition for science or discovery, it would be different, but you did go over the worst part alone and the lower part has been navigated by others, so I would, in your place, let the wild waves kill someone else.[4]

Finally, on September 8, 1933, Herbert Leich wrote to Hal,

When your telegram came we were hoping that you had "your belly full" of river trips. Even if you do complete the trip safe and sound as the first man to do it alone, what will it get you except a newspaper notice which is soon forgotten? Even aviators who do sensational things are not long remembered. Why not be satisfied with being the first man to navigate the upper river? "What price glory?" You will be 25 next Feb. and had better think soon of a permanent career. If you had been here Aug. 1 you might have got a job at the store. . . . I hope you have fully recovered from the effects of your hardships. . . . You might have died of starvation with nobody ever finding it out or might have been stunned on a rock & drowned in the river. Mother has been worrying and dreaming about those very things & used to wake up with a start.[5]

Summing up the family's concern, Leich's mother wrote him in very late 1933 or early 1934, "I hope you won't want to try the trip over again. Now that I know into what danger you ran, I shouldn't have a minute's peace of mind, if I knew you were exposing yourself again to such vicissitudes."[6]

In 1934 Hal accepted a full-time job with the Civil Service Commission as a writer of examination questions, and in 1935 he moved to commission headquarters in Washington, DC, where he remained (except for U.S. Navy service during World War II) until his retirement in 1972 and his death in 1981.

NOTES

FOREWORD

1. It should be noted here that the Colorado River was called the Grand River up until 1921. Historically, the Grand and the Green Rivers met in southeastern Utah—in what is now Canyonlands National Park—to form the Colorado River. Hence the names Grand Lake, Grand Valley, Grand Mesa, and Grand Junction, all places in Colorado associated with the river. In 1921, the Colorado legislature, chagrined to note that their namesake river was nowhere to be found within the state's boundaries, got a bill passed through Congress officially changing the name to the Colorado River.
2. Milligan has done exhaustive research on the history of Westwater Canyon, resulting in his encyclopedic history, *Westwater Lost and Found* (Logan, Utah: Utah State University Press, 2004).
3. John Weisheit, veteran Cataract Canyon guide, author, and one of the leading experts on the history of the canyon, believes after extensive research that Hal lost the *Dirty Devil* somewhere just above Rapid 28. So the "take-out" noted on the accompanying map was not a take-out in the normal sense of a beach or boat ramp, but rather the place his voyage abruptly ended
4. "Shipwrecked in Cataract Canyon," by Harold H. Leich, *Deseret News*, February 13, 1949.
5. The author of this foreword would like to thank Dr. Dawn Amber Dennis of California State University–Los Angeles for her assistance in conducting research on the correspondence between Harold Leich and Otis "Dock" Marston in the latter's extensive archival collection at the Huntington Library, San Marino, California.

CHAPTER ONE

1. Lewis R. Freeman, *Down the Yellowstone* (New York: Dodd, Mead, 1922).
2. Hal Leich, "To the Yellowstone—1930," *American Whitewater* 20, no. 3 (March/April 1975), 63.

CHAPTER TWO

1. Clyde Eddy, *Down the World's Most Dangerous River* (New York: Frederick A. Stokes, 1929).

2. Frederick Samuel Dellenbaugh, *A Canyon Voyage: The Narrative of the Second Powell Expedition Down the Green-Colorado River from Wyoming, and the Exploration on Land, in the Years 1871 and 1872* (New York: Putnam, 1908).

3. Julius Frederick Stone, *Canyon Country: The Romance of a Drop of Water and a Grain of Sand* (New York: Putnam, 1932).

4. Ellsworth Leonardson Kolb, *Through the Grand Canyon from Wyoming to Mexico* (New York: MacMillan, 1914).

5. Lewis R. Freeman, *The Colorado River* (New York: Dodd Mead, 1923), and *Down the Grand Canyon* (New York: Dodd, Mead, 1924).

6. Robert Follansbee, *Upper Colorado River and Its Utilization* (Washington: GPO, 1929).

Chapter Three

1. John Wesley Powell, *Exploration of the Colorado River of the West and Its Tributaries* (Washington DC: U.S. Government Printing Office, 1875), 3.

2. Henry Gannett, *The Origin of Certain Place Names in the United States* (Washington: GPO, 1902).

3. Clarence King, *Geological and Topographical Atlas Accompanying the Report of the Geological Exploration of the Fortieth Parallel Made by . . . A. A. Humphreys* (New York: Bien, 1876).

4. John MacGregor, *The Rob Roy on the Baltic: A Canoe Cruise Through Norway, Sweden, Denmark, Sleswig Holstein, the North Sea, and the Baltic* (London: Low & Marston, 1867); *The Voyage Alone in the Yawl Rob Roy, from London to Paris and Back* (London: Low & Marston, 1868); *The Rob Roy on the Jordan, Nile, Red Sea, and Gennesareth* (New York: Harper, 1870); and *A Thousand Miles in the Rob Roy on the Rivers and Lakes of Europe* (London: Sampson, Low, Marlowe, 1892).

Chapter Four

1. Quoted in Wallace Stegner, *Beyond the Hundredth Meridian: John Wesley Powell and the Second Opening of the West* (University of Nebraska Press, Lincoln and London, 1982), 83.

2. *Report of Committees of the Senate of the United States for the Second Session of the Forty-Fourth Congress, 1876–77,* no. 624, January 31, 1877 (Washington, DC: GPO), 3.

Chapter Five

1. Wallace Earle Stegner, *Beyond the Hundredth Meridian: John Wesley Powell and the Second Opening of the West* (Boston: Houghton Mifflin, 1953), 83.

Chapter Seven

1. "Trip Thru Westwater Canon Was Like Tickling Dynamite With a Lighted Match—Wow!," *Grand Junction Daily Sentinel,* September 28, 1916, reprinted in Mike Milligan, *Westwater Lost and Found* (Logan, Utah: Utah State University Press, 2004), 233–37.

2. Harris Thompson, Elliott Coues, and George Brown Goode, *Exploration of the Colorado River of the West and Its Tributaries: Explored in 1869, 1870, 1871, and 1872, under the Direction of the Secretary of the Smithsonian Institution*, vol. 917 (Washington DC: U.S. Government Printing Office, 1875), 58.

Chapter Eight

1. Ellsworth Kolb and Emery Kolb, "Experiences in the Grand Canyon," *National Geographic*, August 1914, 99–184.
2. Smithsonian Institution, John Wesley Powell, Almon Harris Thompson, Elliott Coues, and George Brown Goode, *Exploration of the Colorado River of the West and Its Tributaries: Explored in 1869, 1870, 1871, and 1872, under the Direction of the Secretary of the Smithsonian Institution*, vol. 917 (Washington DC: U.S. Government Printing Office, 1875), 62–63.
3. James Russell Lowell, *Fireside Travels* (New York: Thomas Y. Crowell, 1906), 123.
4. Julius F. Stone, *Canyon Country: The Romance of a Drop of Water and a Grain of Sand* (New York, London: G.P. Putnam's Sons, 1932), 75.
5. Ellsworth Kolb and Emery Kolb, "Experiences in the Grand Canyon," *National Geographic*, August 1914, 157.

Chapter Nine

1. Clyde Eddy, *Down the World's Most Dangerous River* (New York: Frederick A. Stokes, 1929).
2. Smithsonian Institution, John Wesley Powell, Almon Harris Thompson, Elliott Coues, and George Brown Goode, *Exploration of the Colorado River of the West and Its Tributaries: Explored in 1869, 1870, 1871, and 1872, under the Direction of the Secretary of the Smithsonian Institution*, vol. 917 (Washington DC: U.S. Government Printing Office, 1875), 67.

Chapter Ten

1. Zane Grey, *Robber's Roost* (New York: Grosset & Dunlap, 1932).

Afterword

1. Marcella Jacobi Leich to Harold Herbert Leich, July 1930 (letter postmarked Evansville, Indiana, July 26, 1930).
2. Marcella Jacobi Leich to Harold Herbert Leich, July 1930 (letter postmarked Evansville, Indiana, July 31, 1930).
3. Marcella Jacobi Leich to Harold Herbert Leich, possibly August 1933 (letter is undated; no envelope).
4. Marcella Jacobi Leich to Harold Herbert Leich, possibly August or September 1933 (letter is undated; no envelope).
5. Herbert Leich to Harold Herbert Leich, September 8, 1933.

6. Marcella Jacobi Leich to Harold Herbert Leich, possibly late 1933 or early 1934 (letter is undated; no envelope).